Vasconcelos of Mexico

The Texas Pan American Series

José Vasconcelos, 1955

Vasconcelos of Mexico

PHILOSOPHER AND PROPHET

By John H. Haddox

UNIVERSITY OF TEXAS PRESS, AUSTIN AND LONDON

199

V 332 h

The Texas Pan American Series is published with the assistance of a revolving publication fund established by the Pan American Sulphur Company and other friends of Latin America in Texas.

m N

Printed in the United States of America
by the Printing Division of The University of Texas, Austin
Bound by Universal Bookbindery, Inc., San Antonio

Preface

At the time of his death in June, 1959, José Vasconcelos, whose endeavors in his native Mexico ranged from politics and education to philosophy and letters, was accorded a position of eminence among Latin American philosophers by his fellow Latin Americans. The Mexican philosopher Agustín Basave, for example, speaks of Vasconcelos as "the legitimate glory of the Spanish-speaking world," noting that he is *the* genius of Spanish America.

However, outside this orbit the scholarly world has shown little interest in his philosophical teachings. Very few of his writings have been translated into English; moreover, almost no information concerning him, his philosophy, or—for that matter—Latin American philosophy in general, is to be found in our standard philosophical reference works, whether histories, dictionaries, or encyclopedias.

Vasconcelos created a complex, subtle, and sophisticated philosophical system (including a theory of knowledge, a metaphysics, an ethics, and an aesthetics) which he termed an "aesthetic monism"; yet he was always vitally interested in the proximate realities and the more or less remote possibilities of Mexico, in the character of the "cosmic race" of his homeland, in the "emotive philosophy" which it could create, and in the relations between the Mexican nation and others of this hemisphere which he called "Bolivarism."

There is no "angelism," no "separated intellect," in this philosopher. José Vasconcelos was, in the traditional Spanish phrase, *un hombre de carne y hueso* (a man of flesh and bone), a philosopher who sought truth as the fruit of a total experience, sensory, intellectual, volitional, emotional; he sought the "whole" truth as a "whole" man.

The major works in which he presents both his system of aesthetic monism and his sociopolitical doctrines were written over a substantial period of time—from *Pitágoras* (published in 1916) to *Todología* (published in 1952)—and lesser works were published before and after these dates. Yet, despite minor inconsistencies, the elaborate system of aesthetic monism as expressed with variations in several books has an overall unity, and the principles and spirit of this system also pervade the sociopolitical doctrines he expounded in several other books.

If Parmenides is being-intoxicated and Spinoza is God-intoxicated, José Vasconcelos is unity-intoxicated. Oswaldo Robles has spoken of him as a "cosmic soul" with a *simpatía universal* who has immersed himself in the entire ocean of reality.

Here, emulating this spirit, I have attempted to achieve an inclusive and unified picture of the thought of the Mexican philosopher in its entire range—a range that attempted to encompass everything on earth and in heaven as well.

In Appendix C there are nine selections from Vasconcelos' *Ética, Estética, Tratado de metafísica,* and *Lógica orgánica* in English translation. Although they are brief, I feel they will suffice to illustrate his synthetic style of thinking and his poetic mode of expression.

Special thanks are due the following persons at The University of Texas at El Paso: to President Joseph M. Ray and Deans Clyde E. Kelsey and Ray Small for their encouragement; to Professor John M. Sharp and Rafael J. González for their assistance in translating many of the rich, poetic, and sometimes difficult works of José Vasconcelos from Spanish into English; to my colleagues in the Department of Philosophy (especially to Professor C. C. Crawford) and the members of the Inter-American Institute for their support and inspiration; and to the Organized Research Committee for funds with which I pursued this study.

I also wish to express my appreciation to Dean C. L. Sonnichsen, Monsignor Henry D. Buchanan, Professor Patrick Romanell, Reverend Andrew Burke, Professor John M. Sharp, Professor Lonnie D. Kliever, and John Finnegan for their painstaking reading of the manuscript and their helpful suggestions; to Señor Enrique Vasconcelos for providing me with otherwise unavailable original source materials; to *The Personalist*, the *International Philosophical Quarterly*, and the *Inter-American Review of Bibliography*, published by the University of Southern California, Fordham University, and the Pan American Union respectively, in which some parts of this book originally appeared; and, finally, to Carmen—for everything.

JOHN H. HADDOX

Contents

Vasconcelos of Mexico

1. Patriot–Educator–Philosopher

*J*osé Vasconcelos was born in Oaxaca, Mexico, on February 27, 1882. His father worked for the Mexican government and for much of José's childhood the Vasconcelos family lived in seaports and border towns.

Young José at a very early age showed a propensity for philosophy. He asked questions unusual for one so young: "What am I?" "What is a human being?"[1] To the question, "What is a philosopher?" his mother replied: "A philosopher is one who depends upon the light of reason to discover the truth. A sophist is one who defends what is false, for his personal interests or simply for pride and vanity."[2] José Vasconcelos was never to forget these words.

After attending grammar school (at, among other places, Eagle Pass, Texas), he traveled to Mexico City where he attended the National Preparatory School. In 1905 he received his licentiate in law from the School of Jurisprudence.

As a student Vasconcelos had supported Mexican President Porfirio Díaz and, for a time, apparently accepted the teachings of Positivist philosophy as presented by a group of ideologists for Díaz called the *científicos*, the party of the scientists. This was natural enough, considering that for almost José's entire youth President Díaz had been in power and that all aspects of Mexican

[1] José Vasconcelos, *Ulises criollo*, in *Obras completas*, I, 308.
[2] *Ibid.*, p. 324.

life, cultural and educational as well as economic and political, were controlled by the President and his followers.

During the tenure of President Díaz (from 1876 to 1911, with one four-year interregnum) foreign capital came to dominate the economic life of Mexico, with the ownership of natural resources, many industries, and much of the land taken over by American, British, Belgian, French, German, Spanish, and Canadian interests. Thus, although productivity in Mexico was manifestly greater than before the Díaz regime, much of the profits left the country and what remained in Mexico tended to improve the lot of the already rich rather than help the rural peon or the urban poor.

These facts, plus the suppression of political opposition, led to widespread unrest. Thus, when Díaz announced in 1909 that he was running for office once again, Francisco I. Madero's battle cry *"Sufragio efectivo; no reelección"* won enough popular support to make the overthrow of Díaz inevitable.

In the area of philosophy, Positivism was the ideological bulwark of the Díaz regime. The teachings of Auguste Comte, French founder of the Positivist philosophy, had been introduced into Mexico by the educator Gabino Barreda. In 1868 he opened the National Preparatory School as a center for Mexican Positivism, which, in one form or another, was the dominant philosophical mode of thought until almost 1910. Like Comte, Barreda saw Positivist philosophy, with its denial of metaphysics and theology and its exaltation of science, as the necessary instrument of social progress.

In 1892 the *científicos*, led by Justo Sierra and Francisco Bulnes, justified on "scientific grounds" the fourth re-election of Díaz, the so-called honest tyrant. Now the doctrines of Comte were modified by certain teachings of Charles Darwin and Herbert Spencer. The *científicos* argued: Darwin had shown that in the struggle for existence the fittest survive; Porfirio Díaz had survived three elections; hence he was obviously the most fit to rule in his homeland.

By the time Vasconcelos graduated from law school he was ready to join those opposed to the dictator. This was more than a mere change in political allegiance: he saw Positivism not only as a defense of the dictatorship of Díaz but also as an instrument for the expansion of economic interests from the United States, for the "Anglicizing" of Mexico, and for the development of an empiricist-materialist philosophy.

On October 28, 1909, a group of approximately fifty young intellectuals, led by Antonio Caso, Pedro Henríquez Ureña, Alfonso Reyes, and José Vasconcelos, came together to form the Ateneo de la Juventud. This organization had as its goals the destruction of the Díaz regime, the removal of foreign economic controls in Mexico, and the lessening of the influences of Positivism on the cultural life and educational system of Mexico. Thus when the revolution against Díaz broke out in 1910, these Mexican thinkers attempted to formulate both an ideology of revolution and a plan for the cultural rehabilitation of the nation after the revolt.[3]

At a meeting of the Ateneo in 1910 Vasconcelos presented a lecture entitled "Don Gabino Barreda y las ideas contemporáneas" in which he questioned Barreda's denial of artistic and metaphysical values and his excessive faith in the scientific method. He concluded: "The Positivism of Comte and Spencer could never satisfy our aspirations."[4]

Vasconcelos then became a propagandist for the forces of Francisco I. Madero, who opposed Díaz. Eventually he had to flee to Washington, D.C., where he remained as a confidential agent for the Maderistas. After Díaz was overthrown, Vasconcelos returned to Mexico. This was the beginning of a long and active political career. Oswaldo Robles has noted that if Plotinus exercised a pro-

---

[3] Edith Flower, "The Mexican Revolt against Positivism," *Journal of the History of Ideas*, X (January, 1949), 115–129.

[4] Antonio Caso *et al.*, *Conferencias del Ateneo de la Juventud*, p. 7. For an excellent discussion of the activities of the Ateneo de la Juventud see Patrick Romanell, "Bergson in Mexico: A Tribute to José Vasconcelos," *Philosophy and Phenomenological Research*, XXI, 4 (June, 1961), 501–513.

found influence on the thought of Vasconcelos, it was Plato (with his ideal of a philosopher-king) who inspired his activities.[5]

In 1920, after brief periods as acting rector at the National University and as director of the National Preparatory School, he began one of the most successful periods of his life. That year he was appointed Minister of Public Education by President Álvaro Obregón. As Minister, he was in charge of three areas: schools, libraries, and fine arts. Because of his tireless efforts to reorganize and extend the educational system of Mexico and raise the general level of Mexican education, Vasconcelos has been credited with being the father of public education in Mexico.

He established rural schools in areas where none had ever existed, and these schools were also used as community centers in numerous villages and cities. More schools were constructed during his few years as Minister than in the previous fifty years—more than one thousand rural schools between 1921 and 1924. Thousands of inexpensive editions of the world's classics were published and distributed throughout Mexico. Several anti-illiteracy drives were initiated and cultural movements were encouraged, including a revival of popular arts. Vasconcelos was generous with commissions for the muralists Diego Rivera and José Clemente Orozco. Under the previous President, Venustiano Carranza, 1 per cent of the national budget had been allotted to education; by 1923, due largely to the hard work and enthusiasm of Vasconcelos, this was increased to 15 per cent (and of a larger budget).

Speaking of the great movement in Mexican education at that time, Octavio Paz writes: "It was a social effort, but one that required the presence of a man who could catch fire and then transmit his enthusiasm to others. Vasconcelos, as a philosopher and a man of action, possessed that unity of vision which brings coherence to diverse plans, and although he sometimes overlooked

---

[5] Oswaldo Robles, "José Vasconcelos, el filósofo de la emoción creadora," *Filosofía y Letras*, XIII, 26 (April–June, 1947), 14.

details, he never lost himself in them. His work, subject to a number of necessary and not always happy corrections, was the work of a founder, not of a mere technician."[6]

Vasconcelos' political career did not end when he left this office. He ran unsuccessfully for the governorship of the state of his birth, Oaxaca, and then, in 1929, for the Presidency of Mexico.

Here, as elsewhere, there are apparent contradictions in Vasconcelos' words and actions. In his *Ulises criollo* he speaks of himself as "a solitary,"[7] and in *La tormenta* he affirms his ambition "to grasp everything in all directions—thought, emotion, and action,"[8] less as a philosopher than as an inventor. Yet he felt compelled to labor in the exhausting, years-consuming, often unrewarding field of politics.

Thus Vasconcelos was ever torn between two careers, that of a philosopher and that of a politician. He preferred the breadth of philosophical enquiry to the more limited area of politics, but, as he notes in one of his autobiographical works, *La tormenta*, he always thought it was his patriotic duty, even more, his duty simply as a man, to do his part "to make the environment in which his life is spent cease to be that of a cannibal tribe and to convert it to the purposes of civilization."[9]

There were, then, two reasons for Vasconcelos' involvement in Mexican politics, one negative and one positive. On the one hand, he felt it his duty to resist the "triumph of the wicked, the imbeciles," in Mexican politics,[10] to oppose corruption and tyranny in his country. On the other, he clearly felt from an early age that it

[6] Octavio Paz, *The Labyrinth of Solitude*, p. 152. In *Mexico, the Challenge of Poverty and Illiteracy* Ramón Ruiz presents an extensive analysis of the major role that Vasconcelos played in the struggle against ignorance and illiteracy in Mexico.

[7] Vasconcelos, *Ulises criollo*, in *Obras*, I, 541 (*A Mexican Ulysses*, translated by W. Rex Crawford, p. 50).

[8] Vasconcelos, *La tormenta*, in *Obras*, I, 1016 (Crawford translation, p. 121).

[9] *Ibid.*, p. 1099 (p. 137).

[10] *Ibid.*, p. 992 (p. 118).

was his duty to work for better living, working, and cultural conditions for the Mexican.

As a youth Vasconcelos had participated in the titanic struggle against Porfirio Díaz partly because of the latter's repeated re-elections to the presidency. When he now saw that Plutarco Elías Calles was in effect running for re-election (an action outlawed by the Constitution of 1917), using Pascual Ortiz Rubio as his puppet, he felt compelled to run for the office himself. What apparently started as a gesture of defiance rapidly grew into a full-blown campaign.[11] It started in Nogales on November 10, 1928, when he demanded effective suffrage and no re-election. Despite what seemed to be an extremely successful campaign, he went down to overwhelming defeat—at least according to the official returns, which gave Ortiz Rubio almost 2,000,000 votes to Vasconcelos' approximately 111,000. It was doubtless a fraudulent election; Calixto Maldonado, one of the leaders of the *Antire-elecionista* party, declared: "Democracy has been assassinated; there were no elections." The party president, Victorio Góngora, hopefully proclaimed that Vasconcelos had actually won a majority of the votes, hence was President-Elect of Mexico.[12] Yet hopes for the eruption of another rebellion in Mexico, like that which deposed Díaz, were short-lived. Vasconcelos now left his homeland with an armed escort.

Of this period, G. T. Nicotra di Leopoldo has written: "It is said, in attempting to discredit him, that he was exiled from his native land, that he had to flee his country. Did not Dante, Bolívar, Victor Hugo, and Unamuno also have to flee and for the same reason? Exile for these great men was an honor. Vasconcelos had

---

[11] Vasconcelos' presidential campaign is described brilliantly by one of his aides, Mauricio Magdaleno, in *Las palabras perdidas*.

[12] John W. F. Dulles, *Yesterday in Mexico: A Chronicle of the Revolution,* p. 476. Some frustrated supporters of Vasconcelos insisted that he would have won an honest election, but no one else has seriously suggested this.

a quality of character that was inflexible, loyal, steadfast in rectitude."[13]

Even after this bitter experience the Mexican patriot hesitated to leave politics. In *El proconsulado*, the last of his autobiographical works, Vasconcelos writes: "I felt distressed at the thought of my notes on Ethics lying abandoned in the bottom of suitcases that were constantly moving about. And of the time that I still had to give to the sterile, stupid struggle of Mexican politics; but that struggle was something I was honor-bound to carry on, and was the only way to redeem the sacrifice of those who had died for the regeneration of our country."[14]

Finally disillusioned with politics, he devoted his efforts in the nineteen thirties, forties, and fifties to the creation of an all-embracing philosophical system. At last he could bring to fruition concepts which had been germinating for many years. He could now read and write philosophy as never before. He later remembered with pleasure the hours spent at the New York Public Library on Fifth Avenue and at the Library of Congress in Washington. Of this period Oswaldo Robles writes: "Exiled, José Vasconcelos followed his road with a soul open to all beauty and to all the values of human culture; yet he always maintained a living protest against the forces of imperialism."[15]

Later, after a change in the Mexican administration, Vasconcelos returned from the United States. He was then involved in many activities in Mexico—lecturing at the Colegio Nacional, writing books and newspaper and magazine articles, running a private preparatory school, and directing the National Library of

---

[13] G. T. Nicotra di Leopoldo, "José Vasconcelos: el hombre y el filósofo," *Todo*, No. 1398 (July 23, 1964), 29.

[14] Vasconcelos, *El proconsulado*, in *Obras*, II, 51 (Crawford translation, p. 270).

[15] Oswaldo Robles, "José Vasconcelos," *Revista Mexicana de Filosofía*, II, 3 (1959), 16.

Mexico. He died on June 30, 1959, widely acclaimed as one of Mexico's greatest and most original thinkers.

In 1959 an entire issue of *Revista Mexicana de Filosofía* was devoted to José Vasconcelos, and in it several philosophers are profuse in their praise of his thought. Yet he was, and is, disliked intensely by many of his contemporaries because of his social and political theories and activities.

However, controversial figure that he may have been, no one can accuse him of pettiness. Agustín Basave, in *La filosofía de José Vasconcelos*, remarks that the man evokes memories of the giant figures of the Old Testament and Shakespeare.[16] Truly he was a man larger than life; everything he did, he did on a grand scale.

He was a complex, passionate, sensitive, searching, even tormented figure. At times bitter and acrimonious, he despised the petty tyranny and not so petty corruption in Mexican political life and with vehemence gave written vent to his spleen, as in his scathing denunciations of such figures as former Presidents of Mexico—Venustiano Carranza ("he was deaf and blind, stupid and dumb, and so mad about commanding that he would listen to no advice") and Plutarco Elías Calles (termed simply "a savage") —and of military leaders—Francisco (Pancho) Villa ("an ignorant ferocious type . . . like a wild animal that gets its claws on machine guns and cannons") and Emiliano Zapata ("blind, unconscious, bloody").[17]

Yet he loved with an even greater passion. He loved his children ("a treasure which is a living, changing miracle," he said); he loved Mexico; he loved beauty; he loved artistic and poetic creation; he loved personal integrity and honor; he loved God.

Thus Vasconcelos exclaims: "To me, as to Job, life has given the

---

[16] Agustín Basave, *La filosofía de José Vasconcelos*, p. 17.

[17] The descriptions of Carranza and Villa are from *La tormenta*, in *Obras*, I, 798 (Crawford translation, p. 94), while those of Zapata and Calles are from *El desastre*, in *Obras*, I, 1240 (Crawford translation, p. 155) and 1437 (Crawford translation, p. 186).

experience of knowing infinite happiness and exhausting pain. In the rhythm of my tragic story complaint and rejoicing alternate."[18]

As he once noted: "I have spent half of my life traveling,"[19] and he did visit many lands (including Latin American nations, the United States, England, France, Spain, Italy, Egypt, Israel, and India) in the course of his political career, especially during periods of exile from Mexico. But even more important was his spiritual odyssey. He was ever driven by a desire to achieve a perfect, absolute, and total wisdom, and the difficulties along the way were manifold.

In *El desastre* Vasconcelos remarks: "Every time I have fallen into the trap of amorous obsession, including matrimony, a voice from deep within me has accused me of betraying my calling, which from the cradle has been that of a hermit."[20] Yet clearly a hermit he was not.

At least until his retirement from politics and to some extent even after, his reading in philosophy, though very wide-ranging, was sporadic, disorganized, and at times hurried, hence superficial; and his writing, while beautiful and stimulating, was at times not all that a scholar might desire. For one thing, he was not always careful about identifying his source materials.[21]

This, however, did not really bother him very much because, as noted before, Vasconcelos considered himself an inventor, a creator, and not at all a pedantic philosopher.

[18] Vasconcelos, *El proconsulado*, in *Obras*, II, 10–11 (Crawford translation, p. 227).

[19] Vasconcelos, *La tormenta*, in *Obras*, I, 1108 (Crawford translation, p. 138).

[20] Vasconcelos, *El desastre*, in *Obras*, I, 1505 (Crawford translation, p. 193).

[21] See Appendix A for a brief discussion of these sources.

2. Aesthetic Monism

*I*n *Ulises criollo,* speaking of some notes he had written on philosophy and art as a young man, Vasconcelos remarks that he was even then moved by "the necessity of finding a key, a formula explaining all life, a system coextensive with the universe"; as he put it: "I suffered from the intoxication, the hypnotism of the Whole."[1] In one of his earliest published philosophical works, *Monismo estético,* Vasconcelos criticizes the fragmentary approaches, the "spiritual plagues," of scientific empiricism, evolutionism, and pragmatism. He proclaims that he wants to organize a system founded on the intuition of synthesis, "the eternal fount of systems."[2] This was clearly more than merely a youthful ambition, an "intoxication," a "hypnotism": it was the driving force behind his every effort to create a philosophy.

Vasconcelos notes on the title page of his *Tratado de metafísica* that his system of philosophy called aesthetic monism will be expressed in three volumes: a metaphysics, an ethics, and an aesthetics,[3] and in the *Ética* he explains that in this system the realms of poetry and of science become one.[4]

Further, Vasconcelos insists that such a cosmic vision cannot be

---

[1] José Vasconcelos, *Ulises criollo,* in *Obras completas,* I, 519 (Crawford translation, p. 47).
[2] Vasconcelos, *Monismo estético,* p. 3 (*Obras,* IV, 9–10).
[3] These were published as *Tratado de metafísica, Ética,* and *Estética.*
[4] Vasconcelos, *Ética,* 2nd ed., p. 47 (*Obras,* III, 693).

created by either rationalists or empiricists. Rationalists do achieve a synthetic view, but it is a synthesis on one level, the conceptual, an abstract "synthesis of the homogeneous"; empiricists achieve no true synthesis at all, merely a collection of unrelated or, at best, loosely related facts that have been observed.

Vasconcelos seeks, rather, a "synthesis of the heterogeneous," a synthesis that respects and in a sense even enhances the variety, the heterogeneity, of the elements united. He notes that reality is composed of qualitatively and substantially distinct elements and he insists that the philosopher must respect these qualitative and substantial distinctions while organizing his experiences into a comprehensive, systematic philosophy.

In the Mexican philosophical journal *Logos*, Vasconcelos remarks that the human consciousness facing the exterior world performs two basic operations: first there is the distinction of one element from another, like black from white, and next there is the operation which seeks to reunite, to integrate, that which thinking has separated. The first of these is easy; the second is much more difficult. As Vasconcelos notes, it is much simpler to take a watch apart than it is to put it back together properly. Further, if we reunite the elements distinguished by our thinking, we ordinarily do this on an abstract, "homogeneous" level. "The difficulty of philosophy begins," he insists, "when the elements of a projected synthesis are not homogeneous, but heterogeneous. . . . What is the secret of the reunion, the unification, the re-integration of heterogeneous elements in their active, vital forms?"[5] This is the principal problem for Vasconcelos.

METHOD AND STYLE

Such a "variety-and-unity" synthesis can only be achieved, Vasconcelos feels, "by a system which is that of artists and mystics."[6]

---

[5] Vasconcelos, "Etapa de armonía," *Logos*, I, 3 (September, 1951), 23.
[6] Vasconcelos, *Estética*, 3rd ed., p. 11 (*Obras*, III, 1115).

In *El desastre* he notes that his book on aesthetics would be the culmination of his intellectual life.[7]

Thus Patrick Romanell has acutely observed that Vasconcelos' faith in nothing but the aesthetic method is analogous to the more common faith among contemporary thinkers in nothing but the scientific method.[8]

This aesthetic method is called a "concurrent method" by which all of the organs of knowing are harmonized. The senses, the intellect, and the emotions collaborate to achieve knowledge. As Vasconcelos expresses it: "The world of the philosopher is to be distinguished from the methodology of experimental science and from all specialized approaches, in that it is not limited to a single criterion but must combine all of them; a philosopher requires a super-criterion. He must constantly compare the discoveries of the mind with those of the senses, and with that which the emotions teach him. . . . No philosophy, then, is valid unless it is based upon the harmony of all facets of universal knowledge, and it is up to the philosopher alone to establish the values and hierarchies which give meaning to the harmony."[9]

To project this comprehensive view of reality Vasconcelos employs a poetic method of exposition.[10] The poet, as an artist, recognizes the essential role of the emotions in the knowing process, and he is the artist who employs a discursive language by means of which he can elaborate and explicate this process.

Thus Vasconcelos remarks that a philosopher must be a "poet

---

[7] Vasconcelos, *El desastre*, in *Obras*, I, 1526 (Crawford translation, p. 196).

[8] Patrick Romanell, *Making of the Mexican Mind*, p. 128.

[9] Vasconcelos, *Tratado de metafísica*, pp. 116, 117 (*Obras*, III, 476, 477).

[10] In his *Ética*, p. 12 (*Obras*, III, 668) Vasconcelos says: "A wise poet, this is a philosopher." Regis Jolivet in *Man and Metaphysics* (p. 65) writes that poetry "translates metaphysical experience, but into symbols and images; feels more than it reasons; sees rather than discourses. . . . The poet reveals to us what we cannot utter, coming as it does from the depths of the heart. . . . The truth is that poetry is metaphysical not of set choice, but, as it were, unwittingly, by the mere fact of its profound and humble concern with an experience which it lives rather than contemplates."

with a system."[11] Agreeing with Miguel de Unamuno that "verse is, without doubt, the natural language of spiritual depth,"[12] the Mexican philosopher feels that the insights of a poet are necessary for a grasp of reality and that the philosopher organizes these. The existing world, he insists, is not clear and simple and distinct as Descartes supposed; so he attempts to create a philosophy that concurs with the general schema of the universe, itself a species of "super-poem," by means of the imagination of the poet thinker.[13]

THEORY OF KNOWLEDGE

Unity, Vasconcelos maintains, is the supreme law of philosophy; but again, it must be a unity which respects heterogeneity—the varied character of the world known and of the faculties by which it is known.

These knowing faculties are the senses, the intellect, the imagination, and the emotions. From the point of view of method he distinguishes four: (1) intellectual, *i.e.*, formal or mathematical logic—an abstract science of the homogeneous; (2) inductive, *i.e.*, the experimental method; (3) ethical, *i.e.*, a consideration of ends as criteria applicable to conduct; (4) aesthetic, *i.e.*, a synthesis of the heterogeneous, by means of the senses, the intellect, and the emotions.[14]

The senses and the intellect are directed to a study of the material world. The senses provide the content, the material, the data for knowledge. The intellect organizes this matter into categories, discovers rules of thought, but is, of itself, cold and empty, analytic, indeterminate, and lacking in vitality, purpose, direction.

[11] Vasconcelos, *Ética*, 2nd ed., p. 55 (*Obras*, III, 699). Thomas Henry Huxley (of all people) once made a comment to the effect that nature is not a machine, it is a poem.

[12] Miguel de Unamuno, *Vida de Don Quixote y Sancho*, in *Obras completas*, IV, 368.

[13] Agustín Basave, *La filosofía de José Vasconcelos*, p. 51.

[14] Vasconcelos, *Lógica orgánica*, in *Obras*, IV, 565–573.

Vasconcelos writes that rational knowing is a continual process of converting the personal to the impersonal and that this is not truly knowing. Genuine knowledge—*el conocimiento verdadero*—presupposes the undiminished, actually the heightened, presence of the personal, which stands in a direct relation with the concrete and many-sided universe.[15] We know as human beings with all our faculties alive, not as pure intellects.

Vasconcelos has almost no confidence in reason alone or what is usually called "logic." He contends that "thinking" is not identical with "reasoning." Reasoning employs abstract concepts; thinking is a concrete operation according to which we coordinate the data of our experience. Vasconcelos thus comments that every philosophy based on generalities and abstractions, every philosophy of mere ideas, is like a crystal globe: beautiful but empty.[16]

However, he asserts that his philosophy is not irrational or illogical in any simple way. "Logic is not contradicted, it is surpassed; but in being surpassed it is also respected."[17]

The problem, Vasconcelos feels, is that logic establishes artificial relations among abstracted elements, while the image establishes a natural organization of the concrete elements experienced. The image captures sensory characteristics in the lower stage of consciousness; in the aesthetic, the suprarational or spiritual stage, the image re-creates the perceived object.[18] The idea, being a

[15] Vasconcelos, *Estética*, p. 113 (*Obras*, III, 1214). In *Todología*. p. 33, he describes his philosophy as "a qualitative synthesis, a gradual organization of our sensations with a unity analogous to a melodic phrase." Vasconcelos, on this point, would surely have agreed with E. S. Brightman that philosophy must begin with a multifaceted experience of "the shining present" comprising "all presently observable consciousness—all sensations, images, reasoning, loves, hates, fears and hopes of Now, all conations, strivings and efforts, desires and aversions" (Edgar S. Brightman, *Person and Reality*, p. 36).

[16] Vasconcelos, *Indología*, in *Obras*, II, 1119. In an article entitled "La tarea del pensamiento," published in *La Antorcha*, I, 10–11 (January–February, 1932), 23, Vasconcelos also calls the abstractions of mathematical physics "a macabre dance of dead formulae."

[17] Vasconcelos, *Tratado de metafísica*, p. 173 (*Obras*, III, 520).

[18] Vasconcelos, *Estética*, pp. 221–224 (*Obras*, III, 1321–1325).

purely formal, abstract representation of the object, impoverishes thinking; in contrast, the image is a representation that enriches the object. The philosopher, as "an artist of totality," tends to use his imagination when ideas are insufficient to organize his experiences. Sensation provides the elements of knowing; the imagination creates an aesthetic arrangement.

The imagination, by means of aesthetic-emotional *a priori* principles, reduces the data of the senses to consciousness, ordering this data in such a way as to produce the enjoyment of beauty. Vasconcelos emphasizes that the truth about objects and their qualities can only be expressed in emotional and sensory forms. This aesthetic knowledge includes both facts and feelings about these facts; and these feelings are most important in our lives—stirring us, attracting us, moving us to act.[19]

Former students of Vasconcelos relate an anecdote that vividly illustrates this thesis. One day, upon entering a classroom in which classes had been held for several months, he asked the students if anyone present could describe the back wall of the room. After they had made a few fumbling, unsatisfactory attempts, he allowed them to turn around, whereupon they discovered two long, jagged cracks, a large, irregular discolored spot, a small window and a smaller shelf. Then he remarked that there would have been no question of such ignorance if a beautiful painting had been hanging on this wall. They would have been attracted by—drawn to—the beautiful object and the pleasure resulting from its apprehension. It would for that reason have been a distraction from the lecture, which, he supposed, was the reason for the generally drab, unattractive appearance of classrooms.

The unifying emotion he at times identifies with love—love with its attracting and unifying function, love by which the lover is drawn to his loved one.[20] In the prologue to the *Estética*,

---

[19] Vasconcelos, *Tratado de metafísica*, p. 163 (*Obras*, III, 512).

[20] In his article "Filosofía-Estética" Vasconcelos says, "We have called our philosophy, Aesthetic, in order to signify that it constructs a fundamental

Vasconcelos paraphrases Dante: "The same love moves souls and the stars," and he insists that, in the realm of the spiritual, love, not rational discourse, is required.[21] This is in the spirit of Unamuno, who, in his *¿Qué es la verdad?*, states that truth is what is believed with one's whole heart and soul.[22]

Thus Vasconcelos clearly distinguishes between knowing by way of reason alone and knowing by the method of an emotion-informed intellect, writing that the first way of knowing separates and analyzes certain aspects of objects known while the second tends to unite and synthesize these aspects. Experience yields the heterogeneous and reason dresses our experiences in abstract concepts, employing them for practical purposes. For example, our experience of a falling object is explained rationally by measuring the distance that it falls and the time that it takes and correlating the abstracted, measured variables, while ignoring the qualitative, experiential aspects of the event. These aspects cannot, then, be restored to a vital unity (that respects their diversity), for here there would be a synthesis on one, a conceptual, level—a synthesis of the homogeneous. Emotion, which tends to attract, to move, to unite qualitatively diverse elements *qua* diverse, engenders an enriched knowledge of the varied world that we experience. By means of emotive knowledge, then, we achieve a type of synthesis of which reason cannot even conceive: a synthesis of the heterogeneous. Here we are on the level of the "concrete universal" according to which the affective intuition of beauty becomes an organ of knowledge.[23]

In a beautiful passage Vasconcelos expresses his disdain of a purely intellectual (here mathematical) approach to reality.

---

unity of the heterogeneous in a synthesis of sense experience, reason, and love" (p. 201).

However, this is not, of course, the only emotion for Vasconcelos. In his *Ética* he devotes Chapter XIX to a classification of emotions.

[21] Vasconcelos, *Estética*, p. 14 (*Obras*, III, 1119).

[22] Miguel de Unamuno, *¿Qué es la verdad?*, in *Obras completas*, III, 704.

[23] Vasconcelos, *Lógica orgánica*, pp. 150–155 (*Obras*, IV, 659–663).

Perplexed at the tremendous riddle of my being among beings, I see the mathematician fragmenting his units, profaning the word "unity" in applying it to the petty and conventional; and I note that then he arranges his units, now in one way and now in another, and thereupon plays with and meditates upon the fixed regularities of a world of his own creation; and though this castle of his own invention is admirable, I realize that he has moved so far away from the natures of things that he will never again be able to grasp them. Returning to reality, we involuntarily think of the gardener who, amidst the splendor of a rose garden, sets himself to counting the bushes; as soon as he does so, the most profound, the most stirring aspect of the sight is shattered. And as with the rose garden, so too is the philosophical conception of the Universe destroyed when the mathematician narrows his criterion and devotes himself to calculating the unimportant.[24]

Vasconcelos is similarly critical of formal logic. In the *Ética* he discusses reasoning by means of an estimation, emotive and qualitative, in which a conclusion is reached because it is just or because it pleases. A decision concerning justice involves a qualitative decision of whether one act is better or worse than another. Emotion arrives at conclusions, not according to the rules of logic (which he calls "prisons"), but through "the estimation, the balance, the rhythm of values."[25] It is true, he admits, that at times the emotions can, and do, err more profoundly than reason; but they also produce triumphs which reason can never achieve.

Concerning aesthetic knowledge, Vasconcelos emphasizes that while science analyzes and decomposes, art synthesizes and recomposes. The ideal of scientific knowledge, he writes, is mathematics; the ideal of aesthetic knowledge is music. Abstract mathematical logic involves a falsification of reality in the sense that such a logic abstracts not only from individually existing objects but from all real existents, since it is concerned only with artificially created mental relations. Thus he distinguishes between the concrete logic

[24] Vasconcelos, *Tratado de metafísica*, p. 127 (*Obras*, III, 484).
[25] Vasconcelos, *Ética*, p. 302 (*Obras*, III, 875).

of art, especially music, and the abstract logic of science. The unity-in-variety characteristic of music is desired, as opposed to the abstract unity of mathematics. Only a logic which handles concrete images in contrast to the logic which handles abstract ideas, only a logic based on imagination, the mind's "synthesizing faculty" par excellence, can give us some contact with the fundamental scheme of things.[26]

In summary, Vasconcelos' position seems to be that genuine aesthetic knowledge starts with sensation but surpasses both sensory and intellectual knowledge, being a suprarational operation by which the knower and the known become one. He thus writes: "While intelligence always arrives at dualism, emotion is essentially monistic. Because of that a philosophy wholly formed and rooted in unity has to be aesthetic."[27]

Only the aesthetic emotion is capable of penetrating to the heart of reality—and this is because reality is itself aesthetic. In aesthetic-emotive knowing there is a unification, an identity of the world with our most intimate nature. Aesthetic thought is a condition of communion with the immense and heterogeneous (but integrated, organized, living) universe. Vasconcelos, then, denies that the abstractions of the intellect can grasp the cosmic energy, the universal rhythm of reality, because the concept presents us with only a separated, isolated skeleton of its object. The aesthetic emotion puts us in contact with the mobility, the living flow, of existence.

Vasconcelos avers, then, that "truth is not only a correspondence between the object and the concept, but also a knowledge of the manner in which the elements of creation are combined in order to engender the individuals of which the Universe is composed."[28]

[26] Vasconcelos, *Ética*, p. 85 (*Obras*, III, 718). See also Patrick Romanell, *Making of the Mexican Mind*, p. 123.

[27] Vasconcelos, *Tratado de metafísica*, p. 173 (*Obras*, III, 520). In *Lógica orgánica*, p. 4 (*Obras*, IV, 544), speaking of his aesthetic logic, Vasconcelos says it can better be called an organic logic because "we know with our whole being coordinated, organically."

[28] Vasconcelos, *Temas contemporáneos*, p. 91.

TRANSCENDENTAL MECHANICS

For Vasconcelos, knowledge requires both a unity, a synthesis, and variety, heterogeneity, primarily because the existent world is basically, in itself, a unified reality with varied forms. In his *Tratado de metafísica* Vasconcelos presents his "transcendental mechanics," the conclusions of which are: (1) in the concept of energy, existence acquires its unity; (2) energy, which is one in essence, obeys diverse rhythms of movement in its various cycles; and (3) the rhythm of movement, the value of existence, and the sense of direction of energy are transformed in each cycle.[29] The concept of energy is the basis for the "monism" in Vasconcelos' "aesthetic monism," while the concept of diverse rhythms is the basis for the qualifier "aesthetic."[30]

A being, for Vasconcelos, is always a concrete existent in which energy may be integrated and coordinated on three different levels —that of inanimate matter, that of a living being, and that of spiritual realities. On each level (or each "cycle") energy changes its rhythm and organization, but the energy is the same throughout the entire process. Vasconcelos' aim is to attain a unified, organic vision of the totality of being, but without sacrificing the distinct characteristics of particular objects.

Here he comes up against the problem which haunts all monistic philosophers: the problem of how one substance can appear in so many and varied forms. Vasconcelos answers that energy (not substance, which he considered to be a static Aristotelian category) appears in diverse forms depending upon the rhythm it possesses.

On each level, due to the varying, organizing rhythm, the whole is a structure richer and more perfect than the parts of which it is composed. In his *Estética*, while showing that the whole has forms

[29] Vasconcelos, *Tratado de metafísica*, pp. 237–244 (*Obras*, III, 570–576).
[30] There is an interesting, though obviously loose, analogy here to Aristotelian hylomorphism, with Vasconcelos' "energy" taking the place of Aristotle's "prime matter" and the former's "diverse rhythms" replacing the latter's "substantial forms."

and functions not possessed by the parts, Vasconcelos presents several examples. He notes that the human body as a whole has characteristics and performs operations that are lacking to the isolated cells, fibers, tissues, and organs; that flesh and psyche are united to make a man; that experience and thought together forge our image of the world; and that even "in the great Whole, action and intelligence are subordinated to love and joy."[31]

Energy, expressed in diverse rhythms, engenders the three basic realms of reality: the mineral, the biological, and the spiritual— "the atom, the cell, and the consciousness."[32]

The Mineral Cycle

On the atomic level, in what Vasconcelos calls "the cosmic, corporeal cycle,"[33] there is uniform, mechanical, non-teleological rhythm—an "act of repetition." Even on this plane the particles— proton, neutron, electron, and others—and their operations are integrated in such a way that they form an organized unity. Here there is, on the lowest level, a "synthesis of the heterogeneous." He further notes that in the combination of atoms, for example hydrogen and oxygen, there results the molecule, here water, which is itself a dynamic synthesis of these two elements.

The Biological Cycle

On the second level, the level of living beings, there is spontaneous, teleological movement, with direction and purpose; and while the source of the movement of the atom is from without, the cell, in contrast, is itself a central source of impulses, and, further, such impulses tend to act and organize to realize determinate purposes such as nutrition and defense.[34] On this plane the organization of

[31] Vasconcelos, *Estética*, p. 18 (*Obras*, III, 1123).
[32] Vasconcelos, *Tratado de metafísica*, p. 180 (*Obras*, III, 525).
[33] *Ibid.*, p. 241 (*Obras*, III, 573).
[34] *Ibid.*, p. 193 (*Obras*, III, 534–535).

the elements is more complex but, at the same time, more perfectly integrated, with more "synthesis" and less "homogeneity" than on the inanimate level. For example, the iron in blood is present in a less determinate form, *as* iron, than the iron in a chemical compound such as iron sulfide.

The Human Cycle

The third and highest natural level is that of the human soul. On this spiritual plane the movement is creative, properly and explicitly aesthetic.

Vasconcelos was extremely critical of contemporary views of man. "Compared with Augustinian introspection, with Thomistic arguments, with Kantian analyses, the empirical psychology of our times sounds like a chatter of barbarians recently imbued with culture. Chaos of partial observations; measures and weights of what is by nature immeasurable and without weight; no principle of order; notions that seem modest, only being minute, in reality audacious and ignorant of the fundamental premises of philosophy; total incapacity to embrace problems as a whole."[35]

These approaches have failed, he notes, because man is a conscious being in whom diverse operations—mental, emotional, aesthetic-coordinative—are integrated.

Further, Vasconcelos insists that only the human being can convert or transform the physical and biological into the spiritual. In the biological cycle there are three types of processes. First are such operations as nutrition and respiration (which are hardly more than physico-chemical). Next are operations, involving the will and a degree of intelligence, aimed at the achievement of particular, limited ends. Finally, with finite ends attained, there are operations tending toward higher ends. From the last of these is born the spiritual personality, which is creative and free. This is the aesthetic level. Here energy is not exhausted upon being used,

[35] *Ibid.*, p. 214 (*Obras*, III, 551).

but increases with use as if it already participated in a divine power.

Vasconcelos deplores the fact that there persists a widespread confusion according to which energy on the aesthetic level is supposed to be disinterested—as if disinterestedness in energy and in the person were not an absurdity, given the tendency of both to seek the Absolute. Thus, while the spiritual operations are free as means, their end is determined.[36]

The Divine Being

In *Todología* Vasconcelos adds a fourth dimension to the three of his metaphysics—the atom, the cell, and the human soul. This is the Divine Person, a principle Who subsists of Himself, acting as a Trinity, Who communicates with all of creation, always retaining His isolation and power, but upon Whom depend all other things.[37] The Divine Being is the one reality transcending the three cycles of energy.

Relations among the Cycle

With respect to the relations among the three cycles or levels of energy, Vasconcelos explains that there are two currents of change, one descending toward disintegration (as in the physical law of entropy) and the other ascending in degree of integration and perfection from mineral to living cell to human soul, with the final end "the return to Absolute Being."[38]

In a chapter of his metaphysics entitled "The Revulsions of Energy," Vasconcelos, describing the three levels of energy as three

---

[36] *Ibid.*, pp. 242–243 (*Obras*, III, 573–574). In the *Estética*, pp. 100–104, he criticizes the Kantian description of the aesthetic response as a disinterested pleasure, insisting that the ends of the spirit are sought in works of art. Later in the same work he notes that aesthetics is never completely free, that the artist is ever searching for means to create works of beauty.

[37] Vasconcelos, *Todología*, p. 114 (*Obras*, IV, 919).

[38] Vasconcelos, *Estética*, p. 17 (*Obras*, III, 1121–1122).

mechanics (the mechanics of the atom, the mechanics of the cell, and the mechanics of consciousness), explains how the transit of energy through each of the three dynamic heterogeneous worlds occurs, and attempts to relate each of the partial processes according to the rhythms which direct and embrace the whole movement.[39] Vasconcelos points out that by its nature energy organizes or tends to organize. The movement from indeterminate, "pure inexpressive flow," to particular, purposive, determined activity is the movement from the atom to the living cell. Then, he writes, "in the aesthetic period, the flow again becomes free, but no longer inexpressive; on the contrary, it is the language of expression itself, the voice of immaterial realities, like music or artistic emotion."[40]

The positive movement from one level to the other tends in one direction. The forces in the atom, the drive of the organic toward life, all inclinations, are but diverse manifestations of the movement of energy toward more complex, yet more completely integrated, rhythms.[41]

However, this movement is not a continuous, evolutionary-type development. For example, Vasconcelos calls the movement from the mineral to the biological a "leap." The shift from a relatively disorganized non-teleological rhythm to an organized ("organic") teleological rhythm is not gradual; it is almost abrupt. The living rhythm surpasses, even contradicts, the inorganic. "The cell is the prodigy, the revulsion, in which is initiated the biological cycle. The culmination of this cycle is the instant in which consciousness creates the representation. With the first representation is initiated the new world of immaterial values. The will begins to move in conformity with invisible but real purposes, without extension but active, and values become successively ethical, aesthetic, and religious: we are in the kingdom of the spirit itself."[42]

[39] Vasconcelos, *Tratado de metafísica*, p. 180 (*Obras*, III, 525).
[40] Vasconcelos, *ibid.*, p. 190 (*Obras*, III, 532).
[41] *Ibid.*, p. 221 (*Obras*, III, 557).
[42] *Ibid.*, p. 241 (*Obras*, III, 573).

These "revulsions," then, are violent changes in the quality of energy, which like creation itself, Vasconcelos feels, require the intervention of God. He also describes them as radical mutations of the rhythms of energy.[43] Yet despite the changes in its "quality" or "rhythm," the energy itself does not change.

Knowledge of the Cycles of Reality

In the *Estética* Vasconcelos summarizes how we know each of the cycles (excluding the divine). We observe physical objects through the senses, arrange the sense data by means of intellectual categories, and use the resulting knowledge in technical or applied sciences.

We perceive biological phenomena, with an emphasis on living operations, in order to learn of our biological needs, such as food, shelter, clothing, and recreation. With this knowledge we organize our lives politically, socially, and economically to facilitate the satisfaction of these needs.

We discover spiritual truths and values by means of ethics, aesthetics, and religion.[44]

Finally, in the *Tratado de metafísica* Vasconcelos attempts to discover the interrelation of the various fields of knowledge and to indicate what each contributes to his whole system of philosophy. He expresses this with a terpsichorean image. "Each discipline formulates its own law as it finds it in its own field and the philosopher weaves and intertwines them just as the gyrations of the dance lead one into another so that the music does not hinder the step but, on the contrary, the tempo harmonizes all the movements to establish the rhythm determining the ever-changing movements of the dancers."[45]

[43] *Ibid.*, p. 176 (*Obras*, III, 521).

[44] These three types of knowledge are summarized in *Estética*, p. 138 (*Obras*, III, 1240). See Appendix B for a more complete classification of fields of knowledge present in *Tratado de metafísica*, pp. 296–297 (*Obras*, III, 613–615).

[45] Vasconcelos, *Tratado de metafísica*, p. 110 (*Obras*, III, 471–472).

ETHICS

In his ethics, Vasconcelos' approach is as aesthetic-emotional as it is elsewhere. He emphasizes that through the senses and the intellect we contact the profile or surface of things; while through emotion we grasp their color and value.[46]

Thus ethics is not based upon reason alone. Vasconcelos insists that any rationalistic ethics involves a hopeless confusion of the good with formal truth. Often the will does not follow the lead of reason, because the conclusions of reason can be mediocre and fail to move the will.[47]

To the *res extensa* of the physical world and the *res cogitans* of the intellectual realm, Vasconcelos adds the *res significans* discovered by emotion.[48]

Moral value is determined, then, primarily in an emotional fashion, by a feeling, a sense of right and wrong; and emotion generally tends in either of two directions: that of utilitarian ethics, which involves the pursuit of individual ends and the satisfaction of selfish desires, and that of aesthetics, which is a non-utilitarian pleasure in the presence of the beautiful. Vasconcelos wants these to be united, in the sense that his ethics is concerned with the satisfaction of one's personal needs and those of others but in an unselfish, non-utilitarian (aesthetic) manner. Thus he terms his desired ethics an "aesthetics of the will."

To create a work of beauty the artist gives a special form to some matter, such as the arrangement of sounds in a symphony or of shapes and colors in a painting. Now our human acts and the events and circumstances of our lives are a kind of matter to which we can give a form. Thus in the *Ética* Vasconcelos writes that in a heroic action or a saintly work ethics and aesthetics become one, with the hero or the saint creating a life of beauty. In fact, at this

[46] Vasconcelos, *Estética*, pp. 51–56 (*Obras*, III, 1153–1159).
[47] Vasconcelos, *Ética*, p. 394 (*Obras*, III, 941).
[48] *Ibid.*, p. 292 (*Obras*, III, 868). See also B. A. G. Fuller, *A History of Philosophy* (3rd ed.), pp. 495–496.

point of unification we move into another, a more noble, realm, for it is godlike for men to transcend the good and evil which is their selfish, narrow concern, and to turn to the intrinsic perfection of the beautiful. When art becomes mystical and liturgical we move to the realm of the most perfect kind of life, which is religious.[49]

There are three types of natural values: biological, moral, and aesthetic. Biological values direct and orient life independently of the conscience; here values are deterministic and purely biological. Moral values assume a free will and possess responsibility; here are conscious, human values. Aesthetic values direct one beyond the natural, animal aspects of conduct toward a transcendental destiny; these values lead directly to the supernatural.[50] Thus the fourth type of value is religious. In the *Todología*, Vasconcelos explains the profound difference between a religious and a natural ethics, noting that in his system a secondary place is assigned to ethics, mainly because salvation depends fundamentally upon grace.[51] Aesthetics is the connecting link between natural ethics and supernatural religion.

The fulfillment of ethics is, in Vasconcelos' view, the transformation of biological energy, which is selfish and utilitarian, into aesthetic energy, which is unselfish and oriented toward the Absolute.[52] He insists that an ethics which is anthropocentric is only an unfulfilled ethics, and that without God a complete ethics is not possible.

The so-called biological values are not real, and while ethical and aesthetic values have a reality, they are properly only preparatory for genuine value, which is mystical and divine and the standard for all other values.[53] This is succinctly put by Vasconcelos in his statement: "Goodness and beauty are found only on the road to God."[54]

[49] *Ibid.*, pp. 311–313 (*Obras*, III, 881–883).
[50] *Ibid.*, pp. 316–317 (*Obras*, III, 885–886).
[51] Vasconcelos, *Todología*, p. 164.
[52] Vasconcelos, *Ética*, pp. 174–175 (*Obras*, III, 785–786).
[53] W. Rex Crawford, *A Century of Latin American Thought*, p. 213.
[54] Vasconcelos, *Ética*, p. 178 (*Obras*, III, 788).

For this reason the chapter of *Ética* entitled "Ética revelada" is of special importance. This revealed ethics, Vasconcelos affirms, proceeds by the illumination of exceptional persons who seek neither terrestrial nor moral, but celestial, ends. The aesthetic is the level of a spirit pervaded with joy. A mystical union with God is but one step beyond this.[55]

The orientation and movement of persons toward an aesthetic-ethics, and ultimately a mystical-ethics, must start, not with economists, not with scientists, but with inspired men of God.[56]

AESTHETICS

It is evident that the problem which the aesthetic-emotional method resolves for the other branches of philosophy—the problem of the synthesis of the heterogeneous—is the problem of aesthetics itself. As Vasconcelos points out: "The artist, without abstracting, incorporates themes in a conjunction in which the significance of the parts is enlivened."[57] For example, the notes of which a song is composed, *as part of the song,* possess a character and a power to elicit an emotional response that are not present in the notes heard in isolation. The song is *more* than the sum of its parts.

The secret of the beautiful, then, consists in the arrangement of diverse elements in such a form that they maintain a vital heterogeneity, achieving, at the same time, a unity founded on certain aesthetic-emotional principles.

These principles are applied to objects to create beautiful forms. Thus Vasconcelos writes:

The problem here is one of form as well as of essence, since emotion does not take on a fully material form, is not realized, except in concrete manifestations which emotion itself determines. Every river delves and

---

[55] *Ibid.*, pp. 428–431 (*Obras*, III, 966–968).

[56] *Ibid.*, p. 447 (*Obras*, III, 978). Before Christianity the greatest figure is Buddha, in the opinion of Vasconcelos.

[57] Vasconcelos, *Estética*, p. 177 (*Obras*, III, 1278).

slowly defines its own bed; each flood leaves its mark along the banks and its own particular channel on the bottom; just so does emotion constantly forge and alter its motifs; but never will the particular motif or the limited form be enough to retain all the contents of emotion. Light cannot penetrate the cracks through which water may leak away; but in a cave the flow of water may be recognized by its mysterious music; light, in contrast, dances where not even clouds may ascend. None of the aspects of the object, none of its elements, no sensible impression, none of the senses, none of the forms of reason, no thought, no partial reality, will succeed in containing or capturing the entire course of the rivers and whirlpools of emotion which give birth to aesthetic creation. Only wonder accompanies the endless beauty of earth and heaven.[58]

Elsewhere Vasconcelos remarks that intellectualists see the spiritual in logic, but that he himself situates it in the "rhythmic-aesthetic" operation that arranges the elements of experience by "the loving dynamism of the soul."[59]

Vasconcelos insists that only art truly expresses human feelings and desires, and that the way we live, the way we think and act, are determined mainly by just these feelings and desires. He notes that a person is not aware of or does not enjoy beauty because he intellectually recognizes an equilibrium or a logical proportion; his awareness and enjoyment are the result of an internal disposition, a spiritual sensibility, adjusted to the organic flow of a beautiful object (a painting, a piece of sculpture, a song, a person, a scene), just as reason is accommodated to the laws of logic.[60]

In a chapter of the *Lógica orgánica* on the logic of art Vasconcelos distinguishes between this logic, which is analogical, rich, fertile, and penetrating, and formal or mathematical logic, which is univocal, petty, sterile, and superficial. The latter employs abstract concepts; the former employs concrete images.[61] (Elsewhere he

[58] Vasconcelos, *Tratado de metafísica*, pp. 115–116 (*Obras*, III, 475–476). This is a striking example of Vasconcelos' poetic method of exposition.
[59] Vasconcelos, *Estética*, p. 215 (*Obras*, III, 1315).
[60] *Ibid.*, pp. 215–218 (*Obras*, III, 1315–1318).
[61] Vasconcelos, *Lógica orgánica*, pp. 295–305 (*Obras*, IV, 767–775).

notes that images are the elements of the aesthetic exercise, and what we call the aesthetic *a priori* method is simply the artistic manner of using such images).[62]

The presentation of the painter's emotions on canvas, the sculptor's in stone, the writer's in words, the composer's in notes— all involve the artistic image. With the imagination we select and construct a vision of reality more accurate than any science. This is the reverse of abstraction, which distorts and impoverishes; the image enriches the content of the object known, "it transforms it with semi-divine power." By applying the emotional-aesthetic *a priori* forms to intelligence the image elaborates sense data. The whole image contains more than its sensory and intellectual parts.[63]

The artist does not seek universal knowledge. For example, the sculptor does not think of man in the abstract; rather, discarding universal insignificance, he endeavors to determine and express concrete particular forms to represent the object. Thus a portrayal of Mars tells us more about a man of war than the abstract concepts "man" and "war."

For this reason Vasconcelos comments: "We know the failure of those sculptures which represent war or knowledge in the abstract, and the poor dramas which in English are known as Everyman, Everywoman. Even in the Spanish theater Justice and Faith are represented in a cold, dead fashion. Above all, these are converted into the inartistic precisely because they follow the logical process of the pseudo-Platonic thesis which supposes that the artist is pledged to achieve the perfection of a universal."[64]

In summary, we contact particular objects with our senses, and with our intellect we abstract universal concepts from the sense data, but only by the joint operation of the senses, the imagination, the intellect, and the emotions are we able, in art, to achieve the concrete universal.

[62] Vasconcelos, *Estética*, p. 215 (*Obras*, III, 1315).
[63] *Ibid.*, pp. 221–224 (*Obras*, III, 1321–1324).
[64] *Ibid.*, pp. 221–222 (*Obras*, III, 1322).

Aesthetic A Priori *Principles*

The aesthetic *a priori* principles are rhythm, melody, harmony, and counterpoint. Rhythm consists in the temporal arrangement or ordering of qualitatively diverse elements in a serial line.[65] This is the simplest aesthetic form; it can be found in the music of the most primitive tribe. Here there is no scale, no melody, simply a repetition at variable intervals—a "synthesis by succession." Aesthetically, then, rhythm is an "arrangement in time, achieving significance in the spiritual."

The "significance" here results from a partial agreement between external rhythms, like those expressed in sound, and internal psychological rhythms; this agreement engenders pleasure. By means of rhythm the spiritual desire to order things in our own way is satisfied.

In the case of melody there is a *sui generis* system of relations between the human sensibility and the objects experienced.[66] Vasconcelos writes that in a melodic series the order of the notes is like the arrangement of the elements in the physical world that cause human pleasure; and the pleasure, for its part, is a natural feeling that is present in us independent of any prior experience. In the presence of certain arrangements of sounds or forms or colors we simply experience a joy which cannot be logically explained or justified.

"A melody," he insists, "is not a simple succession of notes, as a phrase is not a simple succession of words." A melody is composed of notes, as a phrase is made up of words, but both the melody and the phrase must be seen as an articulated unit, an organized whole. Yet Vasconcelos holds that there is an essential difference: the phrase is controlled by a strict logic; the melody is not. The

[65] This and the following treatment of rhythm are found in Vasconcelos' *Estética*, pp. 234–252 (*Obras*, III, 1335–1346).
[66] Melody is discussed by Vasconcelos in *Estética*, pp. 252–259 (*Obras*, III, 1352–1360).

melody consists in an arrangement of sounds which awaken significant pleasures in the soul. These relations are intimate, almost substantial, spiritual relations between aesthetic content and the soul that responds. In contrast to formal logic and the logic of science, this is a "logic of the spirit," a "logic of aesthetic emotion" in which is found an order, a hierarchy, independent of mathematics, physics, and formal logic.[67]

Finally, Vasconcelos distinguishes between rhythm and melody. The former, music of pure rhythm, primitive music, is the first aesthetic step, which "barely speaks of the spirit." In contrast, with melody "the soul awakens and becomes attentive."

Harmony adds a new note: simultaneity.[68] Diverse elements are united (like sounds in octaves) and enriched. Diverse notes, remaining diverse, are joined to constitute a new, more perfect, more vital reality—a reality of beauty.

In combining melodic series into meaningful unions, harmony achieves a simultaneity which, Vasconcelos says, "disconcerts our poor logical attention, so used to handling ideas." This simultaneity follows an absurd logic; yet a world that concurs with the real order of things is created by harmony. The effect on the person is a sensation of well-being resulting from the simple evidence of an essential relationship between our consciousness and the world.

Vasconcelos finally notes that the three elements of the aesthetic operation—rhythm, melody, and harmony—are all related to the key problem of philosophy, which is the unification of the heterogeneous, and that harmony achieves this more perfectly than the other two.

With counterpoint, the synthesis of the heterogeneous reaches

[67] Similarly in the *Lógica orgánica*, p. 154, Vasconcelos comments that melody is not dependent upon the laws of acoustics or of mathematical progression but upon the pleasure elicited by certain vital combinations of sounds.

[68] Vasconcelos' treatment of harmony is in *Estética*, pp. 259–266 (*Obras*, III, 1360–1366).

its most perfect form.[69] It brings the simultaneity of diverse elements into concert, which is analogous to the organic unity of a living being. Vasconcelos emphasizes that, in a composition, counterpoint is not simply an element in the development, like melody or rhythm arranged harmoniously, but a more complete unity of all the parts—a unity giving spiritual joy.

Logic, he stresses, cannot be compared with counterpoint; the one is formal, the other is structural. In counterpoint there is "the glow of the spiritual." The conclusion of the syllogism is abstract. The conclusion of counterpoint is a vital synthesis of the heterogeneous. It is like a symphony made up of diverse rhythms and melodies in a harmonious form.

The most important characteristic of counterpoint as a method is its power to create a whole which surpasses all of its parts. Vasconcelos, then, feels that by means of these artistic processes we exercise a power similar to the redemptive power of grace—which is the power to transform the material into the spiritual.

Later, Vasconcelos explains the relation among all these *a priori* principles, pointing out that the elements of the arrangement of the objects necessary for beauty are given us in the laws of rhythm, melody, and harmony. The combination of the elements in a beautiful object is not a unity of the homogeneous in the form of an abstract syllogism with major and minor premises; it is the coordination of the heterogeneous, as in counterpoint. The syllogism reduces its elements to abstract schemes before it can organize them, but counterpoint combines them in their integrity and makes them richer than before their union.[70]

The Categories of Beauty

In classifying the fields of art Vasconcelos adopts the Nietzschean

---

[69] Counterpoint is explained by Vasconcelos in his *Estética*, pp. 266–271 (*Obras*, III, 1366–1371).

[70] *Ibid.*, p. 362 (*Obras*, III, 1459–1460).

categories of beauty—the Apollonian and the Dionysian—to which
he adds a third—the Mystical.

Apollonian art is classical art in which there is no passion,
nothing extreme: all is rational, serene, moderate, simple, bal-
anced, approximating the Platonic ideal.[71] The typical Apollonian
work of art (a paintiing, a piece of sculpture, a song) "arranges the
parts in a manner that fosters repose." Here melody predominates.
This, Vasconcelos affirms, represents the pagan concept of life and
is the beginning of art, not its end.

With the Dionysian we are situated in the second stage of art, in
which to reason is added a frenzied intuition, a "free and intoxicat-
ing joy," an exalting, passionate drive toward pleasure.[72] Here
there is an emphasis on the will and the passions; rhythm predominates (in poetry, tragedy, symphony). Combined with the Christian spirit it creates a romantic "bridge to the mystical." The
unstable equilibrium of Dionysian art oscillates between the at-
tractions of the sensual and the impulse to the Absolute, "violent
and glorious, vile and sacred."

Finally, the Mystical category is achieved, but only on a supernatural level, since it leads one to an intuition, not an abstract
understanding, of the Absolute by the intervention of grace.[73] Here
art achieves the character of a genuine manifestation or revelation
of God, through the cooperation of the artist, the thinker, the saint,
and the visionary. Vasconcelos affirms that an essential feature of
man is his power to create beautiful forms and that man is the
image and likeness of God precisely because of his ability to re-
create the world.

---

[71] Apollonian art is described in the *Estética*, pp. 290–293 (*Obras*, III,
1389–1393).

[72] See *Estética*, pp. 294–299 (*Obras*, III, 1393–1399), for Vasconcelos'
treatment of Dionysian art.

[73] Mystical art is discussed in the *Estética*, pp. 300–309 (*Obras*, III, 1399–
1408). Vasconcelos insists that beauty requires a "conformity with the divine
order," so in Greek art there is not yet beauty "in the sense of supernatural
joy."

Mystical art involves an aspiration, a movement, "to realize, in eternal manifestations, the impulse of supernatural love." Man, "an atom of the divine," has this function of organizing and unifying sensations, ideas, and emotions in the quest for God.

Here everything is seen in its proper perspective. Here everything attains and reveals its true meaning. Here, at last, is achieved the perfect synthesis of the heterogeneous, or harmony and counterpoint.

This is all summarized beautifully by Vasconcelos.

In the end, artistic composition has for its object the use of the elements of the Universe as symbols of a language which expresses the characteristics of the Absolute. This is what liturgy attempts to do; for this reason liturgy is the last and highest of the Fine Arts.

Aesthetics is a formal science, but with its own proper forms. Its secret is not in sensation, which can be or not be aesthetic; nor is it in pleasure, which can be simply sensual; nor is it in the necessary norms of dialectic. The secret of aesthetics is in the composition of the elements. Aesthetics is the art of arranging heterogeneous things in a way that gains significance in a world of pure happiness which is proper to the soul. Aesthetics thus puts us at the doorstep of existence as Absolute. What is beyond is ineffable. Thus aesthetics ends in the mystical.[74]

GOD

Vasconcelos' thought is inexorably drawn to God. In *Todología* he notes that his theory of knowledge as "coordination" (a term he uses instead of "synthesis of the heterogeneous" in some of his later works) leads him to recognize the existence of a greatest being, an ultimate existence, not expressed as a sum or an equation, but as an Absolute Consciousness who rules and sustains the universe.[75]

Later in the same work Vasconcelos remarks that the main

[74] *Ibid.*, p. 273 (*Obras*, III, 1373–1374).
[75] Vasconcelos, *Todología*, p. 45 (*Obras*, IV, 863).

problem of his aesthetic philosophy is that of coordinating distinct spheres of knowledge in terms of an orientation toward the Absolute.[76]

Thus the end for aesthetics is the end for all philosophy: the end of ends, the Absolute. Yet this end cannot be attained by philosophy alone, but only through supernatural revelation and grace. Vasconcelos writes that to express the mystery of revelation is the end of liturgy, and, as revelation embraces all the orders of existence, terrestrial and celestial, human and divine, liturgy is the means for us to coordinate our life with "the fount of all life, Who is God."[77]

It is apparent, then, that the Mexican philosopher does not clearly distinguish between philosophy and theology. He simply presents a system of Christian thought, and his synthetic view includes *all* sources of knowledge: natural (the senses, intellect, imagination, emotions) and supernatural (revelation and grace).

Vasconcelos describes the Absolute Being as Creator ("The living center of all the coordinations is the Creator of the Universe. . . . God unifies with His person, His consciousness, the Universe which is His creation"[78]), as a Trinity ("In God Himself, the diverse persons—Father, Son, and Holy Spirit—each has His function."[79] "Consciousness is the essence of personality. . . . Consciousness is the apparatus of coordinating being. It is not simple, but complex. Being is simple; consciousness is complex: God Himself is [complex] according to the mystery of the Trinity"[80]), as One ("God is one in the sense which defines the Trinity; one because the Three Persons act as One. . . . This unity is not as the principle of number; one can only define it, then, as an act of coordinating the heterogeneous. . . . The unifying act is, of course,

[76] *Ibid.*, p. 179 (*Obras*, IV, 928).
[77] Vasconcelos, *Discursos, 1920–1950*, p. 214.
[78] Vasconcelos, *Todología*, p. 49 (*Obras*, IV, 867).
[79] *Ibid.*, p. 77 (*Obras*, IV, 896).
[80] *Ibid.*, pp. 111, 112 (*Obras*, IV, 916, 917).

indivisible. . . . The name 'He who is' is the most proper name of God: A Perennial Act"[81]).

Here, Vasconcelos proclaims, is the unity of the heterogeneous in the highest and most perfect sense. As our knowing act involves the operation of the senses, the intellect, the imagination, and the emotions by which we have a unified knowledge of diverse realities, analogously God's creative knowledge and action unify the manifold elements of the universe, and God Himself, as a Trinity, is both one and many—one God and Three Divine Persons—with one action and three functions: creation, redemption, and sanctification.

Furthermore, Vasconcelos carefully avoids pantheism (of which he has been accused). In a paper prepared for the Twelfth International Congress of Philosophy in Venice, he explains that God is the only reality Who is not energy.[82]

The method which he assigns to theology is not logical but emotional, the Franciscan *doctrina del amor,* Pascal's reasons of the heart.[83] As Oswaldo Robles notes, according to Vasconcelos "The world has been created by love; the return to Unity is also the consequence of love. . . . In the descending scale of love is creation; in the ascending scale of love is redemption. . . . Love saves the world: in the supernatural, grace; in the natural, aesthetic emotion."[84]

Finally, in *Todología* Vasconcelos presents a table of categories of being:

(1) A structure within which an impulse operates, an animated energy of purposes tending to maintain an individualized action: the atom.

[81] *Ibid.,* p. 147. (Not included in the *Obras completas.*)
[82] Vasconcelos, "El hombre y la diversidad de la naturaleza," *Revista Mexicana de Filosofía,* I, 2 (1958), 6.
[83] Vasconcelos, *Discursos, 1920–1950,* p. 202.
[84] Robles, "José Vasconcelos, filósofo de la emoción creadora," *Filosofía y Letras,* XIII, 26 (April–June, 1947), 224.

(2) An organic cell possessing a structure and animating force which tends to realize purposes, but not dispersed, rather, aiming toward the integration of the organism.

(3) A consciousness including diverse structures, mental, emotional, coordinative, or aesthetic, aiming toward a coherent mode of integration in the person.

(4) The Divine Person Who supposes: not a whole that is the sum of the parts, as Pantheists think, but Who acts according to a Trinity which communicates with all of creation, always guarding His isolation and power, on Whom depend all other beings.[85]

[85] Vasconcelos, *Todología*, p. 114 (*Obras*, IV, 919).

3. A Synthesis of the Heterogeneous?

$\mathcal{T}$he strong personal, emotional, poetic character of Vasconcelos' philosophy is a source of its charm and appeal, but, at times, perhaps even more a source of confusion. Especially for persons who prefer logical simplicity and clarity of expression it may be difficult—if not impossible—to feel with him, to be touched by or to respond to his poetic prose.

In Plato's *Apology* (22c) Socrates remarks: "Then I knew that not by wisdom do poets write poetry, but by a sort of genius and inspiration. They . . . say many fine things, but do not understand the meaning of them." Vasconcelos seems to have understood what he was saying, but the reader may have some real difficulties. He may be impressed with the beauty and warmth of the Mexican philosopher's writings, but he would likely prefer that these writings display more concern for reason and logical coherence than is apparent.

Vasconcelos is truly a poet with a system. The difficulty is that often the poet dominates the philosopher, so that one can enjoy the insights of the poet without being able to discover the system of the philosopher. Good poetry means more than it says. Unless, at times, a person can see "more than it says" in Vasconcelos' poetic reasoning he may not be able to follow the argument developed.

Samuel Ramos comments that there are doubtless many true

ideas in Vasconcelos' writings but that his system as a whole is a work of the imagination, more worthy of an artist or a poet than a philosopher.[1] (To this kind of criticism Vasconcelos would probably reply: "It is too bad you have these difficulties, but there is nothing I can do about them. Reality is not clear and simple. I suppose I could prepare a perfectly rational, logically coherent philosophy—but this would be an outline, a skeleton, or, to vary the image, a mere shadow of reality. God is not the Great Logician; He creates dynamically. My philosophy may be complex, even mysterious, but so is reality.")

Of course such a reply does not eliminate the very real difficulties attendant to Vasconcelos' approach. Philosophy that proceeds by a "lyric process" puts thinking on a purely evocative, poetic level—beyond refutation but subject to caprice.

VALUE

Vasconcelos does rescue philosophy from the ubiquitous reputation of being impractical and irrelevant to the affairs of life. As was shown earlier in the biographical sketch, in addition to being a philosopher he was a man of action, an educator and political leader. In *¿Qué es la revolución?* Vasconcelos insists that the philosopher must be a non-conformist, a social combatant, a politician. To use William James' term, he was, in this sense, a "tough-minded philosopher."

Miguel de Unamuno once wrote that there are dead truths and there are live truths, or rather—since truth cannot die, cannot be dead—that there are persons who receive certain truths as dead, as purely theoretical, in no way vivifying their spirits.[2]

If there is any one word that describes Vasconcelos' thought it is "living." The truths he seeks are precisely those which vivify the spirit. His thought is vital, not just because of his practical (po-

---

[1] Samuel Ramos, *Historia de la filosofía en México*, pp. 134, 135.
[2] Miguel de Unamuno, *Verdad y vida*, in *Obras completas*, III, 826.

litical and educational) proclivities, but even more because in his philosophy he seeks *not* an objective, disinterested truth, but rather a truth which reflects a proximate delight in beauty and an ultimate search for salvation, for eternal joy.

Emotion, which is the subjective concomitant of the discovery of truth for some philosophers, is for Vasconcelos an instrument required for this discovery. Emotion is not the effect of the achievement of knowledge, it is an essential factor in this achievement.

As has already been shown, Vasconcelos sought knowledge by means of an emotion-informed intellect. George Santayana, whose teachings are often quite divergent from those of the Mexican philosopher, here seems to agree. In *The Realm of Matter* he writes: "Reason is not a force contrary to the passions but a harmony possible among them. Except in their interests it could have no ardour, and, except in their world, it could have no point of application, nothing to beautify";[3] and in *Three Philosophical Poets*: "The life of theory is not less human or less emotional than the life of sense; it is more typically human and more keenly emotional. Philosophy is a more intense sort of experience than common life is, just as pure and subtle music, heard in retirement, is something keener and more intense than the howling of storms or the rumble of cities."[4] (The musical metaphor here is as reminiscent of Vasconcelos as the notion expressed.)

Vasconcelos more carefully distinguishes among the knowing faculties—sense, intellect, imagination, emotion—but he only distinguishes in order to unite. The synthesis is more intelligible after an analysis of the parts. One or another of these faculties can be concentrated upon for practical purposes,[5] but the ordinary know-

[3] George Santayana, *The Realm of Matter*, p. 147.

[4] Santayana, *Three Philosophical Poets*, p. 124.

[5] Susanne Langer has written: "All these inseparable elements of subjective reality compose what we call the 'inward life' of human beings. The usual factoring of that life-stream into mental, emotional, and sensory units is an arbitrary scheme of simplification that makes scientific treatment possible to a considerable extent." Susanne K. Langer, *Problems of Art*, p. 22.

ing process involves all of them because man is not a brute limited to sensory activity, nor is he an angel-like, disembodied intellect, nor a figure of pure imaginative fantasy or blind emotion.

Unamuno once described science as a "cemetery of dead ideas" composed of "cadavers of thought,"[6] noting that it "satisfies increasingly our logical and mental necessities," but does not satisfy our "affective and volitive necessities."[7]

Vasconcelos similarly feels that scientific knowledge is real knowledge, but extremely limited by its method, that is, experimentation and a correlation of measured variables. We may know a great many details about nature from this quantitative point of view; but again, what he sought was a unified knowledge from more than one point of view. In contrast to the science of reason, Vasconcelos sought the wisdom of the heart, the imagination, the senses, and the intellect.[8]

The educated modern man has tended to emphasize more and more that only abstract concepts are of value. Our work becomes more specialized, partial, and abstract all the time. We speculate and reflect and simplify, employing concepts which have been abstracted from the complex and confusing realm of our experience. The practical value of such an operation is obvious and immense. Walter Kerr once observed that it is good to be able to sell four thousand horses without having to bring the horses into the office.

Not only in our work, even in our entertainment, we seem to be moving further and further from the living, the immediate, the concrete. More and more we depend on music via records and pictures via movie or television screens rather than on singers and actors in the flesh. Gerald Vann has commented: "We live in a cellophane age; more and more things come to us at fourth or fifth

---

[6] Unamuno, *Del sentimiento*, in *Obras completas*, IV, 533.

[7] *Ibid.*, p. 544.

[8] Gabriel Marcel in his *Creative Fidelity* insists that the philosopher must base his system on *all* his experience, saying: "Philosophy implies an exaltation of experience, not a castration of it."

degrees removed from their natural state: the canned food and the canned music; the air-conditioned rooms and the potted 'reader's digest'; and life becomes more and more unreal."[9]

Abstract concepts are drawn from the concrete, the immediate, the particular. In this operation we gain knowledge of what the elements of our experience are (in a general way); but what exist are concrete, particular objects. Thus, in a special sense, the abstractive operation moves us away from reality.

Further, to abstract means to ignore, to neglect, some elements of our experience. Abstraction always involves selection and rejection from among the attributes experienced, so it never gives us a complete picture.

William Lynch has brilliantly analyzed the approach of what he calls "the univocal mind." This approach is superficial in that it tends to *reduce* everything, all qualitative and individual differences, to a unity, an equality (in the sense of a sameness), ignoring or destroying the unique character of each individual thing, hence eliminating variety. This is temptingly simplistic: clear and logical but unreal and uninvolved. Lynch complains that "it not merely isolates and externalizes; its whole temptation is to reduce everything, like and unlike, to a flat community of sameness—all in the name of an intelligibility and a type of order that does not and cannot belong to the real world. Instead of trying to handle the difference or submitting it to other faculties that might discover intelligibility in it, it tends in various ways to eliminate the unlike, the different, the pluralistic."[10]

Vasconcelos seeks precisely those "other faculties" described by Lynch. For the Mexican thinker, philosophy is necessarily concrete, synthetic, coordinated, never a univocal philosophy, but one

---

[9] Gerald Vann, O.P., *The Water and the Fire*, p. 13. Edith Sewell in *The Human Metaphor*, p. 23, has commented that the present tendency to combine abstraction and automation resembles the Cartesian method whereby all is reduced to "mathematics and machines."

[10] William Lynch, *Christ and Apollo*, p. 122.

involving an interpenetration of unity and multiplicity, sameness and difference.

Though Vasconcelos avers that the senses, the intellect, the imagination, and the emotions are required for knowledge, the primacy given the emotions is most unusual at a time like the present when many thinkers feel that the emotions, being blind, or at least sensual or self-indulgent, should be ignored as operations unworthy of the term "knowing faculties."

Yet Vasconcelos insists that the emotions play an absolutely essential role in life. Their primary function is to move one or draw one toward an object in knowing, in acting, in being. Speaking of an aesthetic experience or a love experience, Abraham Maslow has remarked: "We may even speak of an identification of the perceiver and the perceived, a fusion of what was two into a new and larger whole—a super-ordinate unit."[11]

For Vasconcelos, also, emotion unifies the perceiver with the perceived in an aesthetic experience, the lover and the loved one in an experience of love.

When a person responds to a beautiful object, he is drawn to the beautiful object and the result is not just knowledge *about* the beautiful object, it is of the object itself. It would be possible, for example, to know a great deal about a painting—its measurements, the physics and chemistry of its colors, the subject matter portrayed, the life of the painter—and yet still *not* have come to know the painting because the aesthetic-emotional response is lacking.

The lover desires to be with the (quite literally) "attractive" object of his love; and the lover, in a very special sense, *knows* his love as he knows nothing else. Love is anything but blind, for Vasconcelos; it is the only way to real knowledge. Thus knowledge is not the fruit of isolated reason.

Furthermore, he feels that love is more than just a personal feel-

---

[11] Abraham Maslow, *Toward a Psychology of Being*, p. 74.

ing. It is essential to his metaphysics. Love is the driving (or, per-haps better, the attracting) force which moves the material world toward life, the living world toward the human, and the human toward the divine. Victoria de Caturla Brú has written that, ac-cording to Vasconcelos, the characteristics of each object reflect "the intensity of the amorous impulse received in its migratory journey from non-being to the plenitude of being."[12]

Before examining the value of his conception of God ("the plenitude of being"), we must consider the importance of Vas-concelos' teachings concerning art and the aesthetic experience. Actually these questions are intimately related since his approach to God is itself aesthetic.

This emphasis on art during a period when its value is denied (or, at the very least, doubted) is almost unique. The Marxists, and most Europeans and Americans, tend to equate human value with utilitarian economic value, while at times paying lip service to art.[13] In such a world Vasconcelos is indeed a *rara avis*.

Further, such value is deemed to be attainable only in some "scientific" way—at least in the sense that the approach is quanti-tative and abstract. Thus the impoverishment of method when poetry and art, on the one hand, and science, on the other, are completely divorced, or, what is more common, when poetry and art are simply forgotten.

Vasconcelos ever insists that poetry and art not only enrich scien-tific knowledge but are themselves sources of the most vital knowl-

[12] Victoria de Caturla Brú, *¿Cuáles son los grandes temas de la filosofía latinoamericana?*, pp. 238–239.
[13] Walter Kerr, in *The Decline of Pleasure*, describes some of the effects of this perpetual pursuit of profit: "The contemporary evidence seems to suggest that something other than an occasional crack-up threatens us, that we are more widely rooted in a contradiction. Even as we hurl ourselves feverishly into more and more work, we are quietly aware of a faintly sickening distaste for the work we must do, the world we must do it in, and the selves we must live with while we are doing it" (pp. 92–93).

edge of all. Abraham Maslow, speaking of the artist, affirms that "he is able to bring together clashing colors, forms that fight each other, dissonances of all kinds, into a unity. And this also is what the great theorist does when he puts puzzling and inconsistent facts together so that we can see that they really belong together. And so also for the great statesman, the great therapist, the great philosopher, the great parent, the great inventor. They are all integrators, able to bring separates and even opposites together in unity."[14]

Vasconcelos notes that in a work of art there are tensions and resolutions, differences and sameness, heterogeneity and unity, and that life itself requires continuous activity whereby the many become one and tensions are resolved. In contrast, any resolution of such tensions in science is on one abstract level, in which case there is unity and sameness but not heterogeneity and difference.

Pierre Teilhard de Chardin, the great French scientist-philosopher-theologian, comments that we must rid ourselves of the prejudice that leads us to contrast unity with plurality as though these were contradictory ideas.[15] He remarks that in certain kinds of associations the union of separate elements does not eliminate their differences; it *exalts* them. True synthesis "does not confound; it differentiates."[16] Teilhard presents several illustrations of this point that sound like some of Vasconcelos': the cells in the bodies of higher forms of life become tremendously complicated, depending upon their function; in human societies the specialization grows ever more intense; in the area of personal relationships friends and lovers must communicate with one another in order to express what is in their minds and hearts.

The authentic resolution that Vasconcelos seeks—in art and in life—is, also, never a simple, logical one. It is suprarational. While admitting that philosophical irrationalism has led to a great deal

---

[14] Maslow, *Toward a Psychology of Being*, pp. 131–132.
[15] Pierre Teilhard de Chardin, *The Future of Man*, p. 52.
[16] *Ibid.*, p. 53.

of nonsense in some philosophers, he surely would deny that the rational is the only (or the best) way of knowing.[17] The fact that the emotions have been misused and abused does not rule out their possible fruitful employment in philosophy and in life.

Though it is widely held that pleasures like those resulting from the sensory and emotional experience of the beautiful in art are somehow less pure, less elevated, than are the isolated operations of the intellect, for Vasconcelos the pleasures of art and the aesthetic experience are themselves a direct stairway to God.

In this he is not alone: St. Thomas Aquinas insisted that no man can exist without pleasure, and St. Augustine, when deciding between the useful and the enjoyable, gave precedence to the enjoyable. In a letter to Jean Cocteau, Jacques Maritain, speaking of art, says that it goes directly and spontaneously to God. "To God not as man's end, not in the moral line. To God as the universal principle of all form and all clarity. From the moment it reaches in its own line a certain level of greatness and purity, art heralds without understanding them the invisible order and glory of which all beauty is but a sign."[18]

[17] Kerr, *The Decline of Pleasure*, p. 256. Earlier in this book Kerr describes an aesthetic experience which, while not strictly irrational, involves something much more than cold logic: "We have submitted our senses and our emotions to an experience; and we have enriched the experience immeasurably by continuing to know it, every inch of the way, as an experience. . . . But if the mind is in perfect possession of its powers all the time that the flesh is tingling and the blood running faster, it is waiting for something. . . . It is waiting, precisely, for the moment when the whole painting, or the whole play, or the whole concerto, has come to the precipice of its completion. . . . Then, as aching rhythms and contending colors and factions as opposed as the Capulets and Montagues cry out for a universal satisfaction that can only be achieved by bringing them all into ultimate, exquisite balance, the mind blinks once, stands back, and sees the balance. In this decisive act of perceiving an order among parts, a harmony in differences, beginnings in ends and ends in beginnings, urgency is resolved and passion spent" (pp. 198–199).

[18] *Art and Faith: Letters of Jacques Maritain and Jean Cocteau*, p. 97. Miguel de Unamuno similarly comments: "In art, in fact, we search for an imitation of eternalization. If in the beautiful the soul calms itself and rests

Vasconcelos believes that the artist discovers the key to direct communication with God through love and beauty. In the joyful response to the beautiful—in art or in nature—there results a profound awareness of an Eternal Source of the harmony, the order, the unity-and-variety of the beautiful.

Thus the aesthetic experience is not a sufficient or an exhaustive end in itself. It is a means whereby an unsuspected, perhaps otherwise never to be disclosed, spiritual capacity in an individual is revealed. Thomas Merton affirms that art "introduces the soul into a higher spiritual order, which it expresses and in some sense explains. Music and art and poetry attune the soul to God because they induce a kind of contact with the Creator and Ruler of the Universe. The genius of the artist finds its way by the affinity of creative sympathy, or connaturality, into the living law that rules the universe. . . . (Art) makes us alive to the tremendous mystery of being, in which we ourselves, together with all other existing things, come forth from the depths of God and return again to Him."[19]

---

and recovers, though the anguish is not cured, it is because the beautiful is the revelation of the eternal" (*Del sentimiento,* in *Obras completas,* IV, 628).

[19] Thomas Merton, *No Man Is an Island,* p. 36.

4. Philosopher-Prophet of Mexico

*J*osé Vasconcelos was never content to be a philosopher concerned with philosophical problems divorced from the world in which he lived; and this world was, for much of his life, the world of Mexican internal politics and external relations. In fact, the social, political, philosophical, and religious spheres were closely interrelated in his life and work. In one of his last works Vasconcelos proclaims: "The evil of contemporary philosophy is the evil of the epoch; it is the split that exists among the diverse potentialities of man. Philosophy has lived divorced from religion and the latter is also divorced from the conditions of sociology and international politics. A return to unity is, thus, the most urgent of our exigencies."[1]

A NATIONAL OR A UNIVERSAL PHILOSOPHY?

Since the time of the Revolution of 1910 in Mexico there has been a continuing effort of scholars there to develop a Mexican philosophy. In his *Making of the Mexican Mind*, Patrick Romanell notes that at the time of this revolution (against Porfirio Díaz) the ideologists had two aims: the recovery of Mexico for Mexicans and the discovery of Mexico by Mexicans.[2] The former, they felt, was necessary because under Díaz much of the wealth of Mexico had

---

[1] José Vasconcelos, *Temas contemporáneos*, p. 92.
[2] Patrick Romanell, *Making of the Mexican Mind*, p. 63.

passed into foreign hands, and the latter was necessitated by the fact that during its almost one hundred years of independence (since the War of Independence from Spain) Mexico had been in almost constant turmoil, and whatever philosophy the newly independent nations possessed was adopted from other nations, hence foreign to the reality of Mexico itself. They insisted that Utilitarianism, borrowed from James Mill and Jeremy Bentham, which José María Luis Mora (author of the Reform Plan of 1833) attempted to apply to conditions in Mexico, could never provide a viable philosophy for that nation; and the same was even more true of the Comtian Positivism which Gabino Barreda, and the Spencerian Positivism which the *científicos,* employed to support the "honest tyrant," President Porfirio Díaz.

As was seen earlier, the members of the Ateneo de la Juventud sought, in the classics of literature and philosophy, ideals for a new Mexico. This desire to develop a philosophy with a truly Mexican perspective, one true to the properly Mexican circumstances, that would express the aspirations and ideals as well as the reality of Mexico, was naturally a concern of José Vasconcelos, who had been a leader of the Ateneo. Thus, although at times he insists that his is not a "Mexican philosophy" in any narrowly nationalistic sense but a perennial philosophy elevated above the vicissitudes of the particular, he still does think it behooves an "emotional race" such as his to develop a philosophy based on the particular logic of the emotions and beauty.[3]

Thus he believes that aesthetic philosophy is the style of thinking most congenial to the "Hispanic temperament," and seeks a

---

[3] In *La Antorcha,* a journal he edited and published in Paris and Madrid during the years of exile after his defeat in the presidential election, Vasconcelos writes: "In summary: to those who object that one cannot think of a Hispanic philosophy but only of a universal philosophy, we answer that we will make it Hispanic so long as we cannot formulate an absolutely universal theory, with the same right that the Germans, the French, and the English have their national school in which they attempt to create a formula that may elevate humanity" (*La Antorcha,* I, 8 [November, 1931], p. 27).

Mexican philosophy along these lines. Also, he is much concerned with a defense of Mexican culture against spiritual, cultural, and economic imperialism; so he attempts, especially in the early part of his career, to have his philosophy embodied in educational, social, and political institutions. He explains that a culture develops out of responses of a race or a people to their environment, and with his emphasis on aesthetics culminating in religion, he defines culture as a poetry of conduct and a movement toward the Absolute. This implies that culture is more than just a technical civilization, that "culture" has some connection with (religious) "cult." Vasconcelos insists that all of Mexico's past inclines the Mexican to prefer the cultural effort to what is merely a matter of civilization,[4] and he notes that his own philosophy is based on the treasures of the national experience. Mexican culture, he remarks, is our own and it must be developed, adding: "No one in submission and to everyone his mission."[5] (This is a play on the words *sumisión* and *su misión*.)

Vasconcelos' personal mission as regards Mexico and Latin America was to be a prophet. In *La filosofía americana*, Francisco Larroyo writes: "The enlightened prophets of America announce the future of the New Continent. More than that: the genuine America is not yet; it will be. The future image of the being of America . . . is, for Vasconcelos, a principle of action."[6]

Further, this action is envisaged by the Mexican philosopher as being basically constructive. In his *¿Qué es la revolución?* Vasconcelos states that in every true revolution there is destruction only on the battleground, and when a revolution becomes a government it must become constructive and work for justice and

---

[4] Vasconcelos, *La cultura en Hispanoamérica*, p. 62. He notes that the Spanish, the Indian, and the Mexican past are all replete with great poets, composers, and painters—but where are the great scientists and technicians?
[5] *Ibid.*, p. 64.
[6] Francisco Larroyo, *La filosofía americana*, p. 165. In *The Labyrinth of Solitude*, Octavio Paz writes that Vasconcelos saw Spanish America "as futurity and newness," not only geographically but spiritually.

peace. Living in a state of revolution is not progress; it is chaos. The first requirement for every true revolution is that it be short and thorough. A prolonged revolution is advantageous only for those who live on it; it is a nightmare for the country in general.[7] Later he insists, "a revolution is the movement for a better way of life" and "a revolutionist is, par excellence, anyone who adds a new treasure to the progress of mankind."[8]

Vasconcelos believed he had two treasures to give to mankind, especially to the mankind of Mexico in particular and of Latin America in general. These treasures were the conceptions of a "cosmic race" and of "Bolivarism."

THE COSMIC RACE

The theory of the cosmic race is discussed in a book with that title (subtitled "Mission of the Ibero-American Race"), in *Indología*, and in *¿Qué es la revolución?*

In the prologue to *La raza cósmica* he writes: "The central thesis of the present book is that the distinct races of the world tend to mix more and more until they form a new human type composed of a selection from each of existent lands."[9] Vasconcelos notes that in Europe a mixture of races (including Greeks, Romans, Gauls, Celts, Tuscans) produced the fount of modern culture,[10] and remarks that (after the United States) the most vigorous nation in this hemisphere is Argentina, where there is a mixture of races of European, largely Mediterranean, origin. (Later he suggests that a relative failure to mix races has been a source of weakness among Orientals).[11]

---

[7] Vasconcelos, *¿Qué es la revolución?*, pp. 91–92.

[8] *Ibid.*, p. 93.

[9] Vasconcelos, *La raza cósmica*, in *Obras completas*, II, 903.

[10] *Ibid.*, p. 905.

[11] Later in this same work (pp. 933–934), Vasconcelos writes: "No present race can claim to be the finished model for all other races to imitate. The Mestizo, the Indian, and the Negro surpass the Caucasian in many powers that are properly spiritual. Neither in antiquity nor in the present has there

Vasconcelos concludes this brief historical survey with these words: "In every case the highly optimistic conclusion which can be derived from these observations is that even the most contradictory mixtures can always be beneficially resolved because the spiritual factor in each serves to elevate the whole."[12]

He is thus very much opposed to any theory that proposes the supremacy of a "pure race";[13] and in *Bolivarismo y Monroísmo* he speaks most contemptuously of the Nazi party in Germany and the Ku Klux Klan in the United States.[14] Contrary to the racist theories, according to which a mixture of bloods is considered to be degenerative, Vasconcelos seeks a vital renovation of mankind by means of a racial synthesis. Thus he speaks of "the white, the Indian, the Negro, and the yellow united in a synthetic ideal which I began to entitle the cosmic race, or the final inclusive race."[15]

Vasconcelos presents the theoretical basis for this ideal in a chapter of *La raza cósmica* entitled "El mestizaje."[16] On the one hand, he notes that—according to the Mendelian laws of heredity— the mating of contrary types will produce diverse and complex variations. On the other, he proclaims that the variations will be superior to those that have existed previously if the mixture of

---

ever been a race that is self-sufficient to forge an authentic civilization. The most famous epochs have been precisely those in which various peoples of different races have come into contact and mixed. India, Greece, Alexandria, Rome—all bear witness to the fact that only a geographic and ethnic universality is capable of bearing the fruits of civilization."

[12] *Ibid.*, p. 906.

[13] *Ibid.*, p. 935. "The fact of the matter is that no race is sufficient to itself, and that mankind would lose, it does lose, every time a race is destroyed by violent means."

[14] This opposition to the Nazi Superman theory is important because Vasconcelos has been accused of certain pro-Nazi tendencies. His apparent support of Germany in the 1930's seems to have been partly because of his strong opposition to Marxism (specifically in its Stalinist form) and partly because of his close personal friendship with the German ambassador to Mexico.

[15] Vasconcelos, *La tormenta*, in *Obras*, I, 1250 (Crawford translation, p. 156).

[16] Vasconcelos, *La raza cósmica*, in *Obras*, II, 906–942.

races is in accordance with the laws of social harmony, sympathy, and beauty. Since this mixture would be brought about, not by violence or force, but through free choice founded on an aesthetic sense and love, it will take some time for the results to appear, but when (and if) they appear they will create a period of true, universal brotherhood among men.

Victoria de Caturla Brú brilliantly summarizes Vasconcelos' theory of the cosmic race, noting that in this racial synthesis the biological and especially the spiritual potentialities of all existent peoples will be harmoniously integrated. She writes: "Inspired by the same artistic genius which marks his philosophical works, he assigns as the law of this process of ethnic fusion an aesthetic eugenics which will be directed by a mysterious sense of pleasure in the presence of the better or more perfect (which has been obscured by the utilitarian and rationalistic forces in present-day society)."[17]

In the chapter of *Indología* entitled "El hombre" the Mexican philosopher is more concerned with Mexico than he was in *La raza cósmica* (in which he presents this theory and applies it to Brazil and Argentina). Here he begins by insisting that the Indian races of Mexico are old, century-tried souls who have experienced victory and defeat, life and death, and all the moods of history.[18] Applying the cosmic race theory, he writes that when two civilizations (such as the Spanish and Indian) meet, one or the other will be predominant, but they both undergo changes; they both lose certain characteristics and gain others. He notes that the same thing that happened to the Spaniard during the Arab invasion happened to the Indian during the Spanish conquest.

Vasconcelos has often been accused of over-emphasizing the Spanish side of Mexican culture. As an example, Rodolfo Nieva in an article entitled "Vasconcelos 'Hispanista'" distinguishes be-

---

[17] Victoria de Caturla Brú, *¿Cuáles son los grandes temas de la filosofía latinoamericana?*, p. 58.
[18] Vasconcelos, *Indología,* in *Obras,* II, 1170–1179.

tween "los mexicanos hispanistas y los mexicanos mexicanistas," exalting the latter and attacking Vasconcelos as an *hispanista*, as one who denigrates the indigenous element in Mexico.[19] Vasconcelos does emphasize that the present condition of the Indian is quite backward and that those who wish to make Mexico into a purely Indian nation are seeking a primitivism that would destroy the country. It is also true that in *La tormenta* he speaks of Spain as "the fountain head of everything we had,"[20] and in *El proconsulado* he characterizes Spaniards as generally "magnificent human beings."[21]

Yet Vasconcelos only opposes an Indianism which does not build on the work of Spain. For example, when he describes his duties as Mexican Minister of Education he says there are three areas: the Schools, the Libraries, and the Fine Arts, and two auxiliary activities: aiding the Indian to enter the current of Spanish culture and bringing literacy to the masses.[22] Later he insists that the racial mixture that is necessary for Mexico's salvation has not had time to bear fruit.[23] This mixture, Vasconcelos believes, *is* Mexico; he points out that some Mexicans are mestizo in blood but all Mexicans are mestizo in culture.

He ends the chapter "Pure Race and Mixed Race" in *¿Qué es la revolución?* by noting that he subscribes to the theory that some

[19] Rodolfo Nieva, "Vasconcelos 'Hispanista,' " *El Universal*, November 29, 1962.

[20] Vasconcelos, *La tormenta*, in *Obras*, I, 772 (Crawford translation, p. 86).

[21] Vasconcelos, *El proconsulado*, in *Obras*, II, 547.

[22] Vasconcelos, *El desastre*, in *Obras*, I, 1251 (Crawford translation, p. 157). Clearly Vasconcelos is more concerned with making sure the Indian learns of and adopts Spanish culture than he is with retaining and fostering elements of the Indian culture in Mexico. His point seems to be that while it is true that the Aztecs and the Mayas once controlled mighty empires and were in many ways highly civilized, this is far in the past; and in the present such cultural elements as language, family customs, artistic styles, and religion in Mexico are overwhelmingly Spanish in origin.

[23] *Ibid.*, I, 1495 (Crawford translation, p. 191).

races develop strengths in one area (like the arts), while others develop in other areas (like commerce); and the conclusion of this theory is favorable to a mestizo type of culture wherein various races tend to compensate for their weaknesses through interchange and assimilation.

Perhaps because he wrote as a prophet, Vasconcelos' hopes for the future in Mexico were much brighter than his estimation of the period of the 1930's, when he wrote most of the works quoted here. Especially after he lost his race for the presidency he was quite pessimistic about the fate of his native land. In *El proconsulado* there are such statements as: "The greatest criminals, the most idiotic leaders, were acclaimed as heroes, exalted as statesmen,"[24] and "my country no longer hurt me in my heart, but rather, made me sick at my stomach."[25] When he was very old Vasconcelos remarked in bitter humor that perhaps it would be more accurate to call his people a "raza cómica" than a "raza cósmica."

Late in his career he was also quite critical of Mexican philosophers. For example, in a preface written for Patrick Romanell's *El neo-naturalismo norteamericano* Vasconcelos remarks that he was surprised to learn that Professor Romanell had written a book on Mexican philosophy (published as *Making of the Mexican Mind*); he sarcastically comments that persons in the United States must be very well off financially if they can spend money on a book about *nothing.*[26]

Yet in *El desastre* the Mexican philosopher writes of "our people's great capacity for culture"[27] and of "all that is best in our civilization, a striving in the direction of the heroic goal of contra-

[24] Vasconcelos, *El proconsulado,* in *Obras,* II, 535 (Crawford translation, p. 274).
[25] *Ibid.,* p. 462 (Crawford translation, p. 264).
[26] Vasconcelos, "Preface" to Patrick Romanell's *El neo-naturalismo norteamericano,* p. 7.
[27] Vasconcelos, *El desastre,* in *Obras,* I, 1386 (Crawford translation, p. 181).

dicting and conquering nature so that the spirit may come to its full flower."[28] He also comments: "In Mexico you have only to scratch the soil to find living roots of the old culture covered over by the barbarity of the government,"[29] and says: "What is the duty of the Mexican, of the patriot? To rally to the defense of his Church, of his tradition, of the very soul of his race."[30]

Thus it is clear that Vasconcelos' attitude toward Mexico is ambivalent, torn between despair and hope—despair, especially in the face of political conditions in Mexico during the 1930's and 1940's, and hope for the future, based upon the religious and cultural foundations of the past and upon his high estimation of the potential of the Mexican.

This hope is also founded on his faith that Latin America is destined to become the home of the first synthetic race of the world.[31] He admits that Latin Americans are not and will never be the superior race of the world, in the sense of the most illustrious or most powerful. He proposes something more noble and more difficult than temporal fame; he proposes a fifth race built upon the foundation of Christian love.

Vasconcelos thus believes that Latin America with its synthetic race has the fated mission of serving as a leaven for the humanity of all nations and all lands. It cannot be a land that proclaims to others, "I am superior, I am all," but a land with an infinite desire for integration and for totality opposed to the "exclusivist creed" of narrow nationalism.[32]

He then prophesies that if Mexico does not offer a home and friendship to all men, another land will serve as the starting place for the cosmic race because "no one can restrict the coming to-

---

[28] *Ibid.*, p. 1505 (Crawford translation, p. 194).
[29] *Ibid.*, p. 1264 (Crawford translation, p. 160).
[30] *Ibid.*, p. 1799 (Crawford translation, pp. 223–224).
[31] Vasconcelos, *La raza cósmica*, in *Obras*, II, 923.
[32] *Ibid.*, p. 937.

gether of peoples, the appearance of the fifth race of the world, the era of universality and cosmic sentiment."[33]

In this way Vasconcelos predicts not the triumph of a single race but the redemption of an integral humanity by means of a vital, unifying Christian love.

In the final chapter of his *Ética* he applies his doctrine of the three types of value—biological, moral, and aesthetic—to society. The biological is a state of war, of struggle, of blind will, of destruction. The moral is a state in which technical organizations and systematic cultures are produced by the intellect directing action. The aesthetic is the constructive summit, the state of sublime vision in which all values are organized and integrated.[34]

In *La raza cósmica*, published several years earlier, Vasconcelos presents a similar but more extensive treatment of these three social states. Here he calls them the material or warfaring state, the intellectual or political state, and the spiritual or aesthetic state.[35] These three states represent a process that, Vasconcelos thinks, is very gradually freeing men from the control of material necessity and little by little turning them to the spiritual.

The first and most primitive period is one in which the mixture of races and bloods has been imposed by force, in which the strong man takes the subdued woman.[36] Even in this period the instinct of sympathy and the mystery of pleasure are present in inchoate form, as is reason—but all are dominated by a brute and primitive will.

In the second period reason prevails, taking advantage of the conquests of the will and correcting its errors. The laws and regulations of social, political, and economic institutions are formed with rational foundations. This period proceeds "according to a

[33] *Ibid.*, p. 937.
[34] Vasconcelos, *Ética*, pp. 622–623 (*Obras*, III, 1106–1107).
[35] Vasconcelos, *La raza cósmica*, in *Obras*, II, 928.
[36] The three periods are discussed on pages 928–936 of the same work.

superficial reasoning and an equivocal wisdom which condemn the mixing of races in the name of a eugenics that, because it is founded on false and incomplete scientific data, has not given valid results."[37]

The third epoch, which is slowly developing, will be one in which the spiritual, creative forces in man are most active. Based upon an aesthetic inspiration that produces happiness, it is almost a godlike life. Passion, here, is not a base sensuality but an exalted love, an immediate aesthetic intuition, a suprarational emotion infused with a divine energy.

Of this period Vasconcelos writes: "If we realize that Humanity is gradually moving toward this epoch of its destiny, we will understand that the work of fusion of the races will be realized in the Ibero-American continent according to a law derived from the enjoyment of the highest functions. The laws of emotion, beauty, and happiness will regulate the choice of a mate with a result infinitely superior to that derived from a scientific eugenics which misses the most important phase, that of love. Beyond this scientific eugenics will prevail the mysterious eugenics of aesthetic pleasure."[38]

Vasconcelos often expresses his feeling that one limiting factor in the formation of an aesthetic-emotive philosophy and a cosmic race in Mexico is the influence from the United States.

Concerning aesthetic philosophy, he complains that North Americans are the heirs of the Industrial Revolution and the Utilitarian and Pragmatic philosophy initiated by Francis Bacon and carried to the present by John Dewey.[39] In his *De Robinsón a Odiseo* Vasconcelos contrasts the Anglo-Saxon progressive-pragmatic (Defoe-Dewey) conception of education as vocational training, which is symbolized by Robinson Crusoe, with the Mexican-Latin

[37] *Ibid.*, pp. 929–930.
[38] *Ibid.*, p. 931.
[39] Abelardo Villegas, "La filosofía de José Vasconcelos," *Revista Mexicana de Filosofía*, II, 3 (1959), 42.

penchant for developing a philosophy of ends, for seeking a general conception of the universe, a metaphysics concerned with "la conquista de lo absoluto" by an aesthetic-emotive method.[40]

Concerning the cosmic race, we have seen that as a youth he opposed the evolutionism of Herbert Spencer which had been adopted by the *científicos* in their support of the rule of Porfirio Díaz. They sought to Anglicize the nation on the assumption that the United States, with more science and industry, was superior to Mexico. Later, as was also noted earlier, he was most apprehensive of the "pure-racism" of the Ku Klux Klan in the United States.

There were other reasons for Vasconcelos' so-called anti-Americanism. He was very much offended by what he considered to be the unwarranted interference of the United States in Mexican affairs, complaining that this nation helped Huerta overthrow Madero and later supported Zapata, not to mention the role that he felt American Ambassador Dwight Morrow had played in his presidential election defeat. Thus he exclaims: "In 1929, Mexico had a single enemy: the Yankee."[41]

Vasconcelos was also critical of many things he observed during his various visits to the United States (including periods of exile). He remarks that he was bothered particularly by the cultural uniformity he encountered; he notes that anyone who knows one city in the United States knows the way of life of a hundred and thirty million inhabitants.[42] Later he complains about the monotony of the scenery: "All the cities, built according to the pattern of New York, have their Broadway, with bright signs announcing the same plays, films, and merchandise. In addition to Broadway, there is always the commercial street, the Main Street made famous by Sinclair Lewis in his novel. And it has been repeated

[40] Vasconcelos, *De Robinsón a Odiseo,* in *Obras,* II, 1497.
[41] Vasconcelos, *El proconsulado,* in *Obras,* II, 147 (Crawford translation, p. 237). He describes Morrow as "short-sighted and bow-legged, lacking the flame of intelligence which is supposed to characterize him."
[42] Vasconcelos, *El desastre,* in *Obras,* I, 1563.

to the point of satiety that customs, foods, ideas are also all the same, cut according to the pattern."[43]

Yet, at the very same time, the Mexican philosopher was enthusiastic about the uniform courtesy and spontaneous generosity of the American people. Standardization and warm-heartedness— these characterized the United States through which he traveled, he remarks.

Vasconcelos was also pleased to discover in California the cooperation of races and nationalities from all over the world: Indians, Negroes, Italians, Mexicans, Frenchmen, Chinese, and Japanese. "Life there is free and genuinely human, and throughout the territory there extend like a smile on the face of nature orchards and gardens thick as a jungle. Christian life, fair and hard-working, produced a kind of benediction."[44]

Now it is interesting to note that even as early as 1925, when his personal attitude toward the United States was not nearly so favorable as when he wrote the autobiographical works here quoted (and when he was still a vigorous opponent of U. S. "imperialism"), he admits in *La raza cósmica* that Latin and Anglo-Saxon cultures do not represent two opposite poles, two irreconcilable extremes; on the contrary, both Mexican and North American cultures are the product of many traditions which are complementary rather than contradictory.[45]

Also, even more impressive was a statement made in a lecture at the University of Chicago one year later to the effect that it is a blessing that this continent is divided among Latins and Anglo-Saxons, for the interaction of our cultures may eventually lead to a mutually desired, higher, richer, spiritual world . . . a true all-comprehending type of civilization."[46]

[43] *Ibid.*, p. 1781 (Crawford translation, p. 221).

[44] Vasconcelos, *La tormenta,* in *Obras,* I, 1125 (Crawford translation, p. 140). On several occasions he also speaks very favorably about the "vigorous and enlightened people" that he met at universities in the United States.

[45] Vasconcelos, *La raza cósmica,* in *Obras,* II, 1278–1279.

[46] *Aspects of Mexican Civilization,* by Vasconcelos and Manuel Gamio, p. 21.

By 1955 Vasconcelos had moved a great distance from his earlier deprecatory attitude toward the United States and her culture. In his *Temas contemporáneos,* published that year, his praise of this land is very warm. He goes so far as to claim that José Enrique Rodó was wrong in having the crude, boorish Caliban represent the North American while having the cultured, sensitive Ariel represent the Latin American. Where, he asks, are Latin America's supposed Ariels? And he replies that such excellent men as Poe, Whitman, and Emerson are from the North, not the South. Thus he comments that Rodó committed the most foolish of sins: ignorant vanity.[47]

BOLIVARISM

Despite this disparaging comment about the state of Latin American culture made in 1955, Vasconcelos never gave up hope for the future of Latin America in general and Mexico in particular. In his same *Temas contemporáneos,* wherein he speaks disparagingly of Rodó's ideas, he also explains that the Latin American nations are behind the United States in progress partly because the former were born prematurely of decadent parents (Spain and Portugal at the beginning of the nineteenth century), while the latter, in a relatively mature state, won her independence from a powerful motherland (England at that time). Thus it will take Latin American nations more time to develop. He also believes that as economic conditions improve, so will the political institutions and the cultural achievements of the Latin American nations.[48]

However, even more than for economic development, Vasconcelos pleads for political unity among Latin American nations—a unity which he feels is actually required for this development. His

[47] Vasconcelos, *Temas contemporáneos,* p. 178. Here Vasconcelos is referring to the classic volume *Ariel* by José Enrique Rodó. This work influenced whole generations of Latin Americans in their attitude toward the United States.

[48] *Ibid.,* p. 181. Here he mentions the terrible effects in Latin America of such things as a widespread laziness resulting from malnutrition.

point seems to be that the *United* States is powerful, while the *dis-united* states of Latin America are weak. In unity there is strength; so in *¿Qué es la revolución?* he expresses his hope that the Spanish-speaking nations of this hemisphere will be good neighbors among themselves as well as to the United States.[49]

In *Bolivarismo y Monroísmo* the Mexican philosopher draws upon the plan for Latin American nations to join in a political and economic union that was originally suggested at a conference of these nations in Panama in 1826 by Simón Bolívar, liberator of large areas of South America.[50] In this book Vasconcelos begins by distinguishing between Spanish Americanism and Pan Americanism. "We call Bolivarism the Spanish American ideal of creating a federation of all the lands of Spanish culture; we call Monroeism the Anglo-Saxon ideal of incorporating the twenty Hispanic nations in a North American empire achieved by the political means of Pan Americanism."[51]

Later he speaks of the confrontation of Spanish America with the aggressive nationalism of European nations and the United States, again attacking both the Nazi party in Germany and the Ku Klux Klan in the United States as secret racist organizations—and, at the same time, urging "the defense of our human patrimony."[52] Thus Vasconcelos considers Bolivarism to be the strongest force to op-

[49] Vasconcelos, *¿Qué es la revolución?*, pp. 29–44.

[50] In *Temas contemporáneos*, p. 129, Vasconcelos hails Bolívar as "the greatest hero of our continent," and says: "Bolívar's fidelity to his race and his religious tradition explains, better than his heroic deeds, the fact that his memory is found to be so profoundly rooted in the nations which reflect his activity" (p. 136).

[51] Vasconcelos, *Bolivarismo y Monroísmo*, in *Obras*, II, 1305. Vasconcelos feels there is a strong kinship among Latin American nations, stating, in *El desastre*, that they are "twenty sister nations bound together by language, religion, race and culture." *Obras*, I, 1234 (Crawford translation, p. 153). In *Discursos (1920–1950)*, p. 184, he exclaims: "Viva México, Viva Argentina, Viva Cuba, Viva Chile; in a grand voice, like a trumpet: Viva Spanish America!"

[52] Vasconcelos, *La raza cósmica*, in *Obras*, II, 1361–1379.

pose the domination of Latin America by either European powers or "the Colossus of the North."

This is not the most important reason, however, for his support of Bolivarism. He feels that the Spanish American nations can best provide the elements required for his desired cosmic culture founded on beauty. As Oswaldo Robles puts it:

> He believed that the nations of Iberian culture possess the aesthetic pathos necessary to engender a spiritual race, a cosmic race, an emotional race to which Keyserling (in his *Meditaciones suramericanas*), following Vasconcelos, assigned a fundamental mission in the future of the world, a world which, after an era of war and political agitation, of civilization in crisis, would be a new spiritual, aesthetic, human world.[53]

Thus, in a movie script written in 1939, the Mexican philosopher has Simón Bolívar proclaiming: "It is a sublime idea to make all the Spanish world a great nation, since we all have the same origin, religion, language, some of the same customs. . . . Federate, federate, here is the solution."[54]

[53] Oswaldo Robles, "José Vasconcelos, filósofo de la emoción creadora," *Filosofía y Letras*, XIII, 26 (April–June, 1947), 214.

[54] Vasconcelos, *Simón Bolívar*, in *Obras*, II, 1741. Vasconcelos realized how difficult the achievement of such a federation would be. In *La tormenta* he complains: "The restoration of the unity created by the Spanish monarchy, but in the modern form of a Society of Nations, a community of people of Spanish speech, including the Philippines: how many people in our continent have the brains to grasp this simple proposal?" *Obras*, I, 756 (Crawford translation, p. 81).

5. A True Prophet of Mexico?

*W*hile José Vasconcelos has been highly respected as a philosopher in Mexico, his career as a sociopolitical leader is clouded by controversy. This is due not merely to the bitter aftermath of his abortive political career, but also to the acidity of his comments about his native land.

His attitudes concerning Mexican social and political leaders are often simplistic, with blacks and whites more apparent than greys. As examples, he sees a man like Plutarco Elías Calles as totally black, while Francisco I. Madero is pure white. Yet he can, upon occasion, see varied shades and hues, as when he considers and evaluates the United States and the Mexican Indian.

Like Socrates, he seeks to tell men the truth about themselves, and there is no easier way to make enemies. He is never afraid of exposing himself to scorn and anger. As a fighter, he is honest and fearless.[1]

Just as the Mexican philosopher's knowledge of the history of philosophy is somewhat limited and his interpretation of this history biased in places, so too his reaction to the events of Mexican history is influenced by personal factors, thus on some issues lacking objectivity. Vito Alessio Robles in *Mis andanzas con nuestro Ulises* comments that Vasconcelos' *Breve historia de México*, pub-

[1] This characteristic of the Mexican philosopher is praised by G. T. Nicotra di Leopoldo in an article, "José Vasconcelos: el hombre y el filósofo," in the magazine *Todo*, No. 1398 (July 23, 1964), pp. 28–29.

lished in 1936, is "ni breve, ni historia, ni de México" (neither brief, nor history, nor of Mexico).[2]

Although he was perhaps at times too much of a visionary, too confident of the power of love as a force to unify the races and nations of the world, he was, in fact, one of the main creators of modern Mexican culture. Octavio Paz admits: "If the Revolution was a search for and an immersion of ourselves in our origins and being, no one embodied this fertile desperate desire better than José Vasconcelos, the founder of modern education in Mexico. His work was brief but fecund, and the essence of it is still alive."[3]

Vasconcelos realized that his ideals of the cosmic race and a "Bolivaristic" union of Spanish American nations would be difficult to effect. Yet this, he felt, was the function of an ideal; it can be continually sought and gradually approximated, though it may never be perfectly achieved.

Of these two ideals, the cosmic race will take much longer to accomplish. José Gaos comments that Vasconcelos' vision of the cosmic race "appears to me to be utopian"; but, at the same time, he also speaks of the "political realism of *Bolivarismo y Monroismo.*"[4]

THE COSMIC RACE?

A basic assumption of the cosmic race theory is the essential equality of all men. This does not mean that all men are presently (or ever will be) equal in the sense of "identical" or "the same." Individual diversity of such things as nationality, race, color, intelligence, and artistic or commercial ability is compatible with an essential unity.

This assumption of the essential unity along with the individual diversity of mankind is traditional in Mexico. It extends back to the sixteenth century when Bishop Bartolomé de las Casas pre-

---

[2] Vito Alessio Robles, *Mis andanzas con nuestro Ulises,* p. 9.
[3] Octavio Paz, *The Labyrinth of Solitude,* p. 152.
[4] José Gaos, *Pensamiento de lengua española,* p. 141.

sented his arguments concerning the rights of the Indians; it has been incorporated into Mexico's various constitutions; it determines policies of the present Mexican government.

For Vasconcelos no race is inferior or superior to another in any general sense. Different races and nations develop strengths in different areas. Yet no race exists that is inherently lacking, not only in the essential human characteristics, but also in special abilities that it can contribute to mankind. This theory that emphasizes the compatibility of racial diversity and human unity contains a significant message for a world torn with racial strife.

Turning from the present and practical to the future and theoretical, there is remarkable support for Vasconcelos' theory in some of the teachings of Pierre Teilhard de Chardin. It is interesting that these two men, whose backgrounds and careers differed greatly (and who obviously do not agree on certain points, such as the role of evolution in human history), should at the same time concur in some of their basic conclusions.

In the last part of *The Phenomenon of Man* Teilhard presents a vision with marked affinities to that of Vasconcelos. "The outcome of the world, the gates of the future, the entry into the super-human—these are not thrown open to a few of the privileged nor to one chosen people to the exclusion of all others. They will open to an advance of *all together*, in a direction in which all together can join and find completion in a spiritual renovation of the earth."[5]

This same idea is expressed at greater length in Teilhard's *The Future of Man*, where he emphasizes that the union of human types tends to bring about differentiation, variety, and spontaneity: "Anarchic autonomy tends to disappear, but it does so in order to achieve its consummation in the harmonized flowering of individual values."[6]

---

[5] Pierre Teilhard de Chardin, *The Phenomenon of Man*, p. 244. Arnold Toynbee also expresses a conviction that there is a process in history moving toward a mixture of all the races.

[6] Pierre Teilhard de Chardin, *The Future of Man*, p. 54.

For Teilhard, as for Vasconcelos, only love is a force capable of joining human beings in a manner which completes and perfects them. Human unity can be achieved only when our ability to love, our power of loving, grows until it embraces all of mankind.[7] The mixing of races, Teilhard insists, must not be forced in a totalitarian way. It must be the fruit of love. Without love it is impossible to escape a mechanical, value-denying standardization, even a spiritual enslavement—"the doom of ants and termites."[8]

Through love our deepest self is enriched in the creative coming together of all the races of men. In a statement strikingly reminiscent of some of Vasconcelos', Teilhard proclaims: "Love is the free and imaginative outpouring of the spirit over all unexplored paths. It links those who love in bonds that unite but do not confound, causing them to discover in their mutual contact an exaltation capable, incomparably more than any arrogance of solitude, of arousing in the heart of their being all that they possess of uniqueness and creative power."[9]

BOLIVARISM?

As was noted before, the achievement of a Bolivaristic union of Latin American nations appears to be less remote than the development of the cosmic race. The former can be brought about by means of a decision of these nations to join in a multinational organization; the latter requires generations of racial mixing.

Vasconcelos feels that the lands of Latin America have a spiritual identity, as well as political and national diversity. He believes

---

[7] Pierre Teilhard de Chardin, *The Phenomenon of Man*, p. 265. He seems to share Vasconcelos' confident hope about the potentialities of love along with his less confident appraisal of its present force, writing: "Christian love is incomprehensible to those who have not experienced it. That the infinite and the intangible can be lovable, or that the human heart can beat with genuine charity for a neighbor, seems impossible to many people I know—in fact almost monstrous" (p. 295).

[8] Pierre Teilhard de Chardin, *The Future of Man*, p. 54.

[9] *Ibid.*, p. 55.

that the latter heterogeneity has been emphasized for too long and that the time has arrived for a recognition of the relative cultural, linguistic, and religious homogeneity of these nations.[10]

He diagnosed, earlier than most, the ailments brought about by hemispheric disunity, but he was fundamentally optimistic about the future of a Latin America composed of nations that desire to cooperate intelligently more than to compete ruthlessly. It was not until many years after Vasconcelos wrote his *Bolivarismo y Monroísmo* that an organization of nations which are both independent (as separate nations) and interdependent (as *members* of such an organization), a system which combines hemispheric unity with national diversity, was formed.

Such an organization, in aspiration and design, if not yet in achievement, is the Organization of American States. This organization, since it includes the United States, extends beyond the boundaries of the ideal that Vasconcelos expressed in *Bolivarismo y Monroísmo*. However, he also enthusiastically supported relations between the United States and Mexico based on the Good Neighbor concept. The O.A.S., then, combines the two approaches to inter-American unity that were strongly favored by the Mexican philosopher.[11]

The problems—social, political, and, especially, economic—facing the nations of this hemisphere are enormous, but at least these

---

[10] Anita Brenner has commented: "As Italians sing and Frenchmen cook, Mexicans relish making things. The universal yen for beauty in visual form is taken for granted to be a need as natural as love and as ancient and accessible as frijoles. It proliferates in everything: from the carefully made arrangements of color and form in the fruit and vegetable markets to the daring of entire buildings covered with mosaic murals" ("A Critics' View," *Atlantic Monthly*, Vol. 213, No. 3 [March, 1964], p. 131). Vanconcelos would surely have agreed with this statement, perhaps replacing the word "Mexican" with the words "Spanish American."

[11] It is important to note that Vasconcelos is not alone in preferring this type of inter-American relations to one in which the United States rigorously applies the Monroe Doctrine to situations in Latin America. In fact the Monroe Doctrine is little respected throughout Latin America.

nations are now aware that they can be solved only by their united efforts.

As prophecy, the dreams of José Vasconcelos have at times failed to materialize. Yet who, in the face of the real and potential accomplishments of the Organization of American States, can deny that he is a true prophet of Latin America? José Gaos has suggested that perhaps one day the inhabitants of the lands of this hemisphere will speak of Vasconcelos as "the father of their spiritual homeland," as "precursor," and as "the genius of his race."[12]

[12] José Gaos, *Pensamiento de lengua española*, p. 143.

6. One, yet Many

*J*osé Vasconcelos was an extremely complex figure, but there was a unity to his vision. He was a personal embodiment of his own ideal, a "synthesis of the heterogeneous" in the flesh, so to speak.

A man of tremendous passion who, especially in his youth, committed errors and injustices, he was admired by multitudes in his native land. His career was multifaceted. He was creator of rural schools, libraries, and cultural missions, politician, statesman, educator, lawyer, philosopher, and mystic.

He was for many years intimately involved in practical politics and spent extensive periods traveling the world over, yet he found time to write over thirty books, plus numerous articles, on a wide variety of topics.

He was, at once, a man of action and a philosopher with, in Agustín Basave's words, "an impatience for the eternal,"[1] so he wrote books which were concerned primarily with philosophical questions (including his *Tratado de metafísica, Ética, Estética,* and *Lógica orgánica*) and others directed to social, political, and educational issues (including *La raza cósmica, Indología, Bolivarismo y Monroísmo, De Robinsón a Odiseo,* and *¿Qué es la revolución?*).

Yet, despite all this variety of activity, there was a remarkable unity of aim, a consistency of goal. This goal was to achieve a total vision wherein all the diversified aspects of reality would be uni-

---

[1] Agustín Basave, *La filosofía de José Vasconcelos,* p. 17.

fied while still diversified. As Oswaldo Robles says of Vasconcelos: "The philosopher does not have the myopic vision of an insect, but the telescopic vision of an eagle. The philosopher knows how to open his eyes to all the regions of existence. The philosophical spirit is not analytic; it is a spirit of synthesis."[2]

In the Mexican philosopher this spirit pervaded every aspect of his thought. It was as true of his view of the cosmic race, a synthesis of diverse bloods and cultures, and of his Bolivarism, a federation of Spanish American nations into one exemplary union, as it was of his metaphysic of aesthetic monism, his theory of knowledge as attained by an emotion-informed intellect, and his ultimate goal of union with God while retaining personal identity.

José Vasconcelos' work as an educator might be ignored by the ungrateful of his native land. His political thought might be neglected. His philosophical teachings might suffer an eclipse. But his vision of a unifying Christian love remains as an enduring vision, a vision without stain or blemish.

[2] Oswaldo Robles, "José Vasconcelos, el filósofo de la emoción creadora," *Filosofía y Letras*, XIII, 26 (April–June, 1947), p. 213.

Appendix A

In his *La filosofía de José Vasconcelos* Agustín Basave carefully traces the influences on the Mexican philosopher (pp. 63–82). They include:

Classic Indian Vedic thinkers with their notions of the unity of the knower and the known via emotive knowledge. See José Vasconcelos, *Estudios indostánicos.* The Indian influences on Vasconcelos are also explained by Genaro Fernández MacGregor in *Carátulas,* pp. 42–43.

Empedocles with his philosophy of coordination.

Plotinus with his monism in which the visible and invisible worlds are progressively joined by the impulse of love. Oswaldo Robles has presented a lucid exposition of Vasconcelos' "Christianization" of Plotinus in "José Vasconcelos, el filósofo de la emoción creadora," *Filosofía y Letras,* XIII, 26 (April–June, 1947), pp. 220–222.

Kant with his notions of sensory-conceptual knowledge by means of *a priori* forms or categories.

Bergson with his anti-intellectualism. For the influence of Bergson on Vasconcelos see Patrick Romanell, "Bergson in Mexico: A Tribute to José Vasconcelos," *Philosophy and Phenomenological Research,* XXI, 4 (June, 1961), 501–513.

Whitehead with his metaphysical system flowing into religion and his organic view of the universe.

Pythagoras with his tendency to base philosophy on ethics and aesthetics—although Vasconcelos rejects the scientific-mathematical side of Pythagoreanism. See José Vasconcelos, *Pitágoras, una teoría del ritmo.*

Nietzsche with his Dionysian and Apollonian categories of beauty, to which Vasconcelos adds the Mystical.

Appendix B

I. Sciences of Nature
   Physics—Dynamics
      (a) Method: Discovery
      (b) Law: Measurable rhythms—Gravitation
      (c) Object: Qualification of existence for its use
   1. Mathematics ⎫
   2. Physics   ⎪
   3. Cosmography ⎪
   4. Geology   ⎪
   5. Geography ⎬ Particular Disciplines
   6. Mineralogy ⎪
   7. Chemistry   ⎪
   8. Mechanics ⎭

II. Sciences of Life
   Ethics—Art
      (a) Method: Invention
      (b) Law: Instinct—Will—Ingenuity
      (c) Object: Quality of existence through notions of emotion for
         its betterment
   1. Biology   ⎫
   2. Natural history ⎪
   3. Physiology   ⎪
   4. Psychology   ⎪
   5. Ethics   ⎪
   6. Medicine   ⎪
   7. Engineering ⎬ Particular Disciplines
   8. Law   ⎪
   9. History   ⎪
   10. Economics   ⎪
   11. Politics   ⎪
   12. Sociology   ⎭

III. Sciences of the Spirit
    Aesthetics—Mysticism
        (a) Method: Emotion
        (b) Law: Fusion, coordinations of heterogeneities in dynamic-
            isms that transcend the particular and temporal. Beauty
        (c) Object: Transfigured existence. Perfection
    1. The Apollonian—Plastic: ⎤
        Painting
        Sculpture
        Architecture
        Music
        Dance
    2. The Dionysian—Literature: ⎬ Particular Disciplines
        Poetry
        Tragedy
        Symphony
    3. The Mystical—Illumination:
        Music
        Philosophy
        Religion ⎦

IV. Science of the Divine
    Theodicy
        (a) Method: Revelation
        (b) Law: Grace
        (c) Object: Redemption of existence and final synthesis of
            knowledge

Appendix C

Some Representative Selections from the Writings
of José Vasconcelos

KNOWLEDGE

From Chapter IV of
Tratado de metafísica
The Method
(*Obras completas*, III, 473–477)

It is of special interest to note that each series of particular disciplines is made up of common elements, and that the only thing distinguishing one from another is an intrinsic distinctive characteristic in the orientation of the movement. In the areas of reality, from the atom to grace, there is a series of broad and concentrated fields, but there is always a substantial unity, a community of existence, and the possibility of their concurrence in the final goal of redemption.

The sensible world, the intelligible, and transcendental reversion, here are the three fundamental categories; the methodological problem is to determine the common connection that allows them to coexist without conflict and, moreover, to concur in a common direction toward liberation. To define the relationship and the manner of transition among the diverse manifestations of existence is one of the purposes of the philosophy sketched in these pages, and our method, as well, must be in accord with this purpose. To show, at the same time, that not only the soul but also nature suffers and rejoices because of this eagerness to transcend itself, is another of the fundamental goals of our doctrine.

Necessary agreement between method and subject matter can only result from the comparison of the reality which is being dealt with and the system which interprets it and orders it. We have already stated that aesthetics gives us a type of dialectic exclusively its own; its aim is to create suprasensible realities and at the same time transmute its external energy. Whether it derives an image from reality or whether it envelopes the object itself in an aura of beauty, aesthetic emotion imposes upon existence its own order and logic, which has always been recognized in old sayings such as "logic of the heart," "the heart has its reasons that reason does not understand," etc.

Its standards—alogical logic, free rhythm, the passion of becoming—go beyond the objective law but without being alien to it, without ceasing to move it and modify it in a fundamental fashion; on the contrary, beauty frequently transfigures the object and raises it to the plane of emotion. According to aesthetic standards, the object enters the realm of the spirit, by dint of the combined witchery of beauty's image, the affinity, and the pathos. At this point, analytical judgment and the image itself become fused in a dynamism of the emotions, which is creative of beauty, just as structure becomes one with energy and maintains it in the atom, and as the body maintains and nourishes conscious life. Reason is to the soul what the body is to the spirit, a framework of fixed movements; we must go beyond it in order to delve into its infinite profundities.

For example, with music the judgment plunges itself into the abyss, where it is dissolved; I am referring to logical judgment; but on the other hand, another model makes its appearance which is, as it were, a sort of more flexible skeleton, a framework accommodated to the new nature, the angelic nature, which one needs in order to live beauty. That other logic is the logic of aesthetic judgment, which unlike the syllogism inclines us to hope for, obliges us to demand, the miracle, the exception, salvation. A similar thing occurs in every poetic judgment, and shines forth in all its splendid power in the enlightenment of those who are profoundly inspired, and even in that of those who are less inspired, as one may note in the first verse of some chapters of the Koran: "In the name of mild and merciful God"—a sovereign cry that thunders as if a golden drum were deafening heaven with its music; wondrous rings expand; celestial trumpets tremble; and their echoes expand space limitlessly. Overhead, the abyss is enraptured with brightness, like an infinity which is but poorly imitated by the domes of the greatest mosques. The air is filled with fragrances, as if the gardens of paradise had opened their gates. "Mild and merciful God"—the resounding vibrancy of these magic words re-echoes, bringing into harmony with themselves all the echoes of creation. . . . True art is always thus, an open sesame that elevates us, with soul rejuvenated, to an improved and transcendental creation.

It has not thus far been possible to formulate the basis for an exact philosophy in which the subject and the object, science and religion, may be brought into harmony rather than into mutual opposition, simply because the aesthetic problem has stood in our way. We still have not been able to define the significance of this problem within the general process of knowing; nor even less, to show how it is a means to grace for the object itself. Therefore, we have frequently been in like error in judging aesthetics either as the goal of the living process or as a simple variant of biological energy. Hence, currently we have applied to it constantly the first logical method, the biological; but never its own, superior because it is genuinely spiritual.

Furthermore, we have time and again, in the case of art, confused form and content; holy creative inspiration needs forms in order to make itself apparent to our nature; but inspiration passes and the form remains; inspiration frequently remains unfulfilled; at other times, inspiration does not succeed in giving life, in transforming its mold, and then the mold reverts to its parallel, the intellectual form subject to the logic of reason, which is the logic of the object. Thus we see, for example, that in the classical Spanish theater the characters frequently discuss their love until they turn it into a dialectic; in the French theater it is even worse, for pathos becomes the golden mean, and one must turn to Shakespeare again to find the lyric tide which elevates the soul and the world beyond the mean, reason, and form.

The problem here is one of form as well as of essence, since emotion does not take on a fully material form, is not realized, except in concrete manifestations which emotion itself determines. Every river delves and slowly defines its own bed; each flood leaves its mark along the banks and its own particular channel on the bottom; just so does emotion constantly forge and alter its motifs; but never will the particular motif or the limited form be enough to retain all the contents of the emotion. Light cannot penetrate the cracks through which water may leak away; but in a cave the flow of water may be recognized by its mysterious music; light, in contrast, dances where not even clouds may ascend. None of the aspects of the object, none of its elements, no sensible impression, none of the senses, none of the forms of reason, no thought, no partial reality, will succeed in containing or capturing the entire course of the rivers and whirlpools of emotion which give birth to aesthetic creation. Only wonder accompanies the endless beauty of earth and heaven.

It is not a simple task to follow art's own law; creative artists are rare, and even they, if they allow themselves to be enthralled by their aesthetic emotion, run the risk of falling prey to passions, dances and orgies, until they are blinded and become as incapable of progress as a Persian Sufi or a howling dervish, despite the fact that their point of departure is sublime emotion. This means that in the human condition one has no right to delay for a long time, and that, hence, to achieve precise philosophical knowledge one must employ a method based upon attentive observation as well as upon a constant motivation toward higher conditions.

At any rate, the world of the philosopher is to be distinguished from the methodology of experimental science and from all specialized approaches, in that it is not limited to a single criterion but must combine all of them: a philosopher requires a super-criterion. He must constantly compare the discoveries of the mind with those of the senses, and with that which the emotions teach him.

Philosophy cannot disregard universal ancient knowledge without falling into the childishness of contemporary empirical systems; neither may it ignore contemporary discoveries relating to the material world and to our dealings with material things; but the supreme law must not be sought in a physical world. As soon as one affirms that practical convenience establishes the law, the instinct to transcend it is destroyed, and the greatest of the powers at philosophy's disposal is precisely the instinct to transcend the material world.

No philosophy, then, is valid unless it is based upon the harmony of all facets of universal knowledge, and it is up to the philosopher alone to establish the values and hierarchies which give meaning to that harmony; the method to achieve such a task must be, accordingly, multifold, and not isolated, but interrelated—both an interlacement of the cosmos and a sign of the spirit that transcends it.

In order to begin to conceive a system, it is fundamental that we recall that each one of the realms into which existence can be broken down possesses its own rhythm of development and perfection, and yet that none of them can by itself explain the universal process. To join the spokes to the hubs one must first observe how the change from one order to another takes place. Reality viewed from within by a judgment participating in its rhythms, but transcending them, reveals to us regular processes and leaps. Whenever existence passes from power to will, from will to enjoyment, and vice versa, judgment is filled with astonishment as if it were in the presence of something that lies without its realm; but emotion understands, and becomes intoxicated with miraculous power; then, under the full power of its own nature, it ascends a scale, the scale of emotions, and sees how, within a single essence, the object is clothed, as it were, in light, in the oppositions of different types of energy; the biological impulse is fulfilled and realized in pleasure, and the feeling of the soul is overwhelmed with divine joy. Here we have a glimpse of unity in the heterogeneous, a unity which takes in the three primary orders: object, intelligence, will.

Since emotion embraces more than intelligence, it is of prime necessity to assign it a place of honor among the means of knowledge. Thus we shall continue investigating and penetrating until we find a supreme unity, which can gather in all the currents without obliterating their identity, in order to bring into being by their means a new mode of existence. One word defines our method: concurrent.

Translated by John M. Sharp and John H. Haddox

From Chapter V of
Tratado de metafísica
Modes of Knowledge
(*Obras completas*, III, 489–491)

Let us now try this definition: emotional knowledge manifests itself when things and processes reveal a sudden identity or disparity with our innermost nature. When we perceive certain processes taking place in the outer world, such as the flow of melody, we feel arising in our consciousness as well a parallel flow, intangible but real, flexible, and almost free. At the same time we become aware that the flow within becomes more closely joined to the flow without, that one can influence the other. Moreover, rational knowledge works upon a substance that is a matter of indifference to me and whose development depends on its own nature, without my being able to change it fundamentally. On the other hand, the flow that I perceive with an internal sense of identity to it seems subject to my free will, and offers me at least the possibility of exerting my free will upon the thing and of affecting it in a parallel fashion.

A certain opposition between the two modes of knowledge, rational and emotional, that is, the one that discovers the rules of a process and the one that inquires into its nature and purpose, is no obstacle to their working cooperatively in the task of research. Pythagoras, without distinguishing the two modes, achieves their synthesis when, after defining the relationships of the triangle and the squares derived from it, and after finding the numerical combinations of the triad, the square, and so forth, he moves on to music to follow in it the development of the numerical rhythms; but it is necessary to note clearly that in the same instant that the move is made from numbers to music, one enters the field of aesthetics and one's judgment is no longer rational but emotional when one enters a realm of knowing through sympathies and differences based on emotion. By difference or by similarity of essence or of goal the two dramatic poles of every aesthetic contemplation are engendered: the subject and the object, no longer confronted for measurement by the rules of logical judgment, but suspended in the mutual mystery that separates them in a sort of morphological reality, while joining them through their involvement with the Absolute.

Numbers themselves become part of aesthetics as a result of emotion whenever music or the dance make of them a sort of internal structure of the pirouette of sound. In this case numbers lose their mathematical or quantitative value and acquire a structural sense; numerical rhythm indicates the index of quality necessary for a process to attain a significance capable of moving us.

Numbers are as subordinate functions of spiritual rhythms; numbers are as signs of the order that the emotions imbue things with so that they may acquire sympathetic reality and development. In approximately the same way, I defined the role of numbers in aesthetics twelve years ago in my essay on Pythagoras; within this interpretation numbers, purely quantitative standards, become the sign of a harmony peculiar to the heterogeneous. No longer will there be subtraction nor multiplication since one is dealing with the heterogeneous—not even the false, provisional homogeneity that is the result of grouping under a number objects distinct in nature but collected together for the purposes of calculation: no formal homogeneity, no predestined regularity. Numbers themselves are on the alert, ready to change their array according to what may come. The order will not be produced by numbers, but will only be marked by them and recorded by them; the key to that harmony will be in them; they will not be its cause, but rather, the record and the mark of its effect. The command that motivates the process does not come from the nature of numbers but from the nature of emotion, from the law of beauty, which is not mathematical, nor physical, nor physiological, but much more than all that: aesthetic.

It is evident, accordingly, that besides rational knowledge, which is a result of the exercise of the intelligence on the data of the internal and external sensitivity, or the sensitivity produced by both, we possess another means for penetrating reality, that is, another mode of knowing. The intuition of color as a scale of beauty, of sound as melody and mystery, the emotion of the presence and correspondence to us of things that are intimately related to us, although superficially farther from us than the water we drink or the air that replenishes our blood, all these experiences constitute a source of a specific type of knowledge that cannot be transferred to another category, but is closely linked to us in a sort of instinctive coordination and existential harmony.

Accordingly knowledge is not a synonym for thought but something still more inclusive than thought; that is, it involves bringing into the terms of consciousness elements that are most extraneous to it, making them part of our lives according to their affinities to the various powers of our personality so that all become joined in an awareness of super-existence and transcendence in which dissimilar elements are combined for the total achievement of harmony. Of course we are not proposing a type of harmony that will respect each unit of reality; on the contrary [we are proposing] a great, perhaps catastrophic, series of deep emotions and changes that will keep changing things, beings, and goals.

Translated by John M. Sharp and John H. Haddox

From Chapter XI of
Lógica Orgánica

Logic of Art

(Obras completas, IV, 769–770, 773–775)

Intellectual knowledge is separative and analytic; it distinguishes the notes of a concept; it reduces reality to concepts, being to structures. Thought by analogy also separates and unites, but as a whole, synthetically; analogy's first stage is as a chemical relationship in which there are still distinct chemicals, but also an integration of the elements that are unified in a compound, even if it has different qualities from the components—for example, the oxygen and hydrogen in water, the nitrogen, oxygen, et cetera in air. This capacity to act without disappearing in the compound and at the same time to collaborate in its formation appears to increase in the realm of the spiritual.

When the mind thinks by analogy, it does not become depersonalized by uniting abstractions like those in arithmetic or geometry; instead it penetrates within things and discovers in them differences and similarities, separations like water and oil when combined, but also compenetrations like those of water and wine, of two persons, of two temperaments, of loves or friendships, of antipathy and repulsion. This way of knowing by analogy is more profound than any intellectual way, and also more fertile.

We will not know any reality if we do not penetrate it with our feelings. We have measured and weighed, formed the equation, the multiple, and the root. Yet he who has not seen the rainbow will not know color. He who does not know about music does not know the soul of things. He who does not sympathize with man will not understand man. This is how one knows that his mind functions in conformity with the Logos, and he who does not love God will never probe the mystery of the Cosmos, nor, properly speaking, of existence.

Now all action is manifested according to the peculiar forms of its development. Discourse cannot proceed without concepts; analogy operates by means of images. . . .

In the process of analogy identity functions without a lessening of existence. The principle of identity is converted into a genetic likeness and originates thought by analogy; its high point we can find in love.

This consummates an identification, imperfect according to form but real, however, in the deepest sense, and fertile because at the same time it unites and separates; one who loves does not wish to disappear in the loved one, like the drops of water in the ocean (according to an unfortunate simile), but wishes to be himself while his loved one continues to be herself. We do not wish to lose ourselves even in God; we would like to conserve the individuality in which we were created, and naturally it would be absurd if we wanted to dissolve ourselves in God, to substitute ourselves for God. Here then is a mystic union that does not destroy the personality but exalts it. It does not lessen the difference, it augments the richness of the conjoined. The sentiment of sympathy among men has the same foundation, only attenuated and at times inverted, in this sense: that as we are imperfect, we do not desire determinate differences or varying substance; we would like to annihilate them within ourselves and in others in order to reap a better type of nature. The miracle by which each person is like others and yet is able to change and develop for others enriches existence for all.

When mathematics develops a number and creates the series 1, 2, 3, 4, 5, et cetera, all the numbers arranged by unity, capable of returning to it, dissociating, disintegrating, it achieves an identity that functions in the abstract and with such notorious poorness that we can follow all of its development. When the principle of identity is employed in the comparison of myself with other selves, of being with beings, it is possible to take note of this principle, and not the developments that, by their infinity, are confused with the universe. It is in thought by analogy that we discover the marvelous nature of the root of the cosmic order that is the inexhaustible relation of Unity and Plurality. Unity as principal creator and constructor. Plurality as the aggregate of its creations. Only the principle of analogy permits us to orient ourselves to these prodigies.

To what point do the similarities of structure permit or aid in the attainment of identities of feelings in the world: man with man, beast with beast? Maybe this is the same as asking the question, Where does the One Being rule and where does the autonomy of His creations begin? There is no created thing to which we are not in some way related; but from a surface view, thought by analogy has no limits and loses itself in the plurality of details. When the mind returns to its focal point and contemplates the Absolute Being, analogy finds its limit, its origin, and its cause. Each being is grasped according to its nature. We think of God by the analogy between His infinite attributes and the attributes of His creatures. His essence is an eternal mystery and we understand it only by means of our capacity to comprehend without fully grasping it. He cannot be an object of *cogitatio*. He can be the object of limitless admiration that broadens and strengthens the conscience, by means of the processes of analogy.

Translated by Carmen and John H. Haddox

METAPHYSICS

From Chapter VII of
Tratado de metafísica
The Revulsions of Energy
(*Obras completas*, III, 570–571)

Conclusions for a Transcendental Mechanics

The mechanics of existence form their laws, then, in the following manner:

First. Unity of existence in the concept of energy.

Second. Energy is one in essence; yet it does not obey the same rhythms of movement in all its manifestations; it first shows itself with uniform movement, then with intentioned movement, tending toward external ends, and lastly with creative movement which invents and carries out transcendental mannerisms. In each one of these cycles the movement is developed in conformity with a peculiar rhythm and passes from one cycle to another by means of leaps or revulsions of energy.

Third. In each cycle, at the time the rhythm of movement changes, the value of existence and the sense of direction of energy also fundamentally transform themselves. The law of movement is primarily Newtonian and Einsteinian, then volitionist, moralist, and then aesthetic, creationist, religious. In general, in order to unroll itself and operate, energy proceeds by triads; each cycle consists of a triad and at its termination it commonly goes out of its cycle to enter the triad of the following cycle.

It cannot be affirmed that the cycles proceed from one to the other by evolution; but it can be affirmed that the lower energy in one of the inferior cycles has to cross the successive cycles, be it slowly or rapidly and be it in a direct or indirect manner by the intervention of auxiliary forces. For example, the human force which transforms physical nature into aesthetic material and the divine grace which elevates the energy of consciousness to the energy of Spirit.

The thesis of evolution is not enough to explain even the development in each of the cycles, much less the passage from one cycle to another.

The cycle of the corporeal we know through the experience of the senses, experience organized by the mind. Considered from our point of view, the corporeal cycle is reduced to sensation and the formal idea; so seen, the first cycle reveals to us the cosmic energy.

The cycle of life we know through direct interior experience confirmed by sensation, a sensation directed by the will. It is very confused, perhaps because in its breast the forces create crises in attempting to go out of materiality and enter the spirit.

We become aware of the cycle of the soul through a recognition of the possibility of situating existence outside the sensibly material planes; this is shown in the following experiences: image immobile or moved by simple biological associations: image incarnated in beauty, incorporated into the law of the spirit; communion with the essentially incorruptible blissful reality.

Translated by John M. Sharp and John H. Haddox

From the Prologue to
Estética
(*Obras completas*, III, 1123)

The Whole, then, is conceived organically; for example, the human body is a whole in relation to the cells, the fibers, the humors of which it is constituted, and further, it possesses that which is not found in any of the parts, or better, the consciousness of a unitary action which serves the parts. . . . A Whole can only be conceived as something more extensive than its parts, and also as having a faculty not possessed by the parts. In this superior capacity the heterogeneous elements find their orientation; for example, the flesh and the psyche are unified to make the man; matter and thought forge our image of the world. The Whole always contains what is not in the parts nor in their sum. The Whole is a structure more elastic, more capable of containing various parts, than the parts which are integrated. A superstructure, we could say, if the word did not have technical senses alien to our meaning. The Whole is a substance in the highest grade of coherence and of existence.

Translated by Carmen and John H. Haddox

ETHICS

From Chapter XIX of
Ética

Classification of Emotions
(Obras completas, III, 874–875)

According to what we have seen, emotion results from the conflicts and actions of forces acting within us and from the diverse influences which form our ethical atmosphere. The three conflicts that we have analyzed —physical, organic, emotional—establish problems which demand solutions. In fact, by their own efforts they succeed in resolving themselves in a third state of final equilibrium, of constructive synthesis. All of the possible solutions manifest themselves according to a dynamic rhythm in one of the following three double categories: mechanical-rational, biological-ethical, and aesthetic-mystical. We may consequently distinguish:

> Solutions: mechanical-rational,
> biological-ethical,
> aesthetic-mystical.

In certain circumstances emotion operates as a syllogism: it raises a conflict, takes a position, and in acting conquers or cedes, but without ever arriving at a strict logical solution; it never deduces a determinate argument, but rather a consideration, an estimation, emotive and qualitative, with only as much intellection as might be desired; a conclusion is thus reached because it is just or because it pleases, never because it is logical, since the mechanics [of logic] have no meaning in this type of judgment. An estimation of justice which involves a decision concerning "worse and better" supposes quality. The resolution of the first conflict in the physical world is called vital by some, but it is preferable to leave this word for biology, so as not to lose sight of the essential fact that emotion operates in an unextended subject matter and with a positive value for the human conscience rather than for the senses. Emotion attains solutions, not according to rules such as those of logic, but through the estimation, the balance, the rhythm, of values. These values, which are virtually plastic at first, become spiritual, immaterial, in the superior processes of emotion. The reason for the acknowledged superiority of the emotive syllogism over the logical syllogism is readily apparent. The powers which come into play are superior, although this does not exclude the possibility of errors even more profound than those committed by reason. On the other hand, they also produce triumphs of being which reason can never achieve.

Translated by Rafael J. González and John H. Haddox

From Chapter XX of
Ética

The Hierarchy of Values

(*Obras completas*, III, 885–886)

The systems of will which are the moral values are referred to as conduct. When it passes from the will to the aesthetic judgment, emotion adopts other systems of fulfillment and of realization. The aesthetic values thus appear to be different, because they do not direct conduct but rather the modes and meanings of enjoyment.

There result three types of values:

The biological values which orient life, before the functioning of conscience.

The moral values which depend on the will and suppose responsibility.

The aesthetic values which surpass the temporal aspects of conduct and direct one to a transcendent destiny.

The passions are the impulses which reconcile themselves with, or separate themselves from, norms and values. If the impulse is in accord with the norms, the transcendental destiny is accelerated and the resulting passion is glorious.

Translated by Rafael J. González and John H. Haddox

AESTHETICS

From the Prologue to
Estética

(*Obras completas*, III, 1115)

Without conforming to the pluralistic empiricism of science, we aspire to an organized and total experience by a system which is that of artists and mystics. This system does not exclude the verification of each premise, but requires continuous efforts for the composition of related elements, not remaining dispersed but integrated in the architecture of a cosmic vision without which there is no philosophy.

Translated by Carmen and John H. Haddox

From Chapter VIII of
Estética
The Aesthetic A Priori

(*Obras completas*, III, 1313–1316; 1318)

Submitting acts to a schema is a tendency natural to the mind and the initial effort of all philosophy. The ancients are believed to have founded the method of philosophy precisely in the attempt to subordinate external processes to the forms of the intellect, in contrast with primitive thought that assimilates the movement of objects within the impulses and desires of our will. The effort of intellectualization and schematization of reality reaches its highest point in Scholasticism. Creation itself is imagined to be the intelligent action of the Divine Mind. From here to the Logical God there remains but the single step that was taken by mistaken Idealists led by Hegel. But while Idealism almost fell by its natural weight, the scientific investigation of reality went about organizing its own method and ended by constituting the *Novum Organum* of Bacon and, with more certainty in our day, the concept of reality derived from mathematical physics. It tells us that reality in its organization, far from being made by syllogisms, is reduced to manifesting certain regularities amidst an incessant instability. The purpose of the present chapter will be to demonstrate that aesthetic activities also obey rhythms and specific regularities and that our consciousness rejoices according to certain mental or spiritual *a priori* principles that are independent of logic and far removed from the simple sensism of empirical aesthetics.

Things go their way, constructing their destiny, and it is not for us to impose upon them a law coming from within the subject, but to discover that law in things themselves. This is what science does; what science discovers is a *sui generis* process, a chain of transits of quantity without any significance for the ends of the spirit; yet, on the other hand, from that apparent indifference we derive the most astounding practical consequences. Man knows that he cannot reduce the exterior world to his mental schemas but he can to his ethical and aesthetic ends. Reality does not lack a schema; what happens is that it has its own, so the schema of material development can collaborate with the work of man. This is what contemporary wisdom tells the individual when he asks: What are things like? Things are in conformity with the sciences that study them by a process rigorously quantitative and without spiritual significance but susceptible of being used for the ends of the individual. Thus we are given a part of the truth, the truth of things and the problem of the agreement between things and the knower. Things are moments of the elemental substance, but we are not; it is nature that codifies substance and gives to us an organized Universe. It is not our intelligence that fabricates the quantity, the arrangement, of substances that constitute the external world. If, then, we do not even suspect, before using experience, how the intimate laws of things are, we cannot continue to imagine what are the mental *a priori* principles that construct external reality for us. The return to Idealism is not plausible, not even as a hypothesis, after the achievements of physics and chemistry. But what, then, are the laws of our intelligence, the principle of identity, the law of contradiction—are they absolute mental operations? What value has an absolute that does not find its counterpart in reality, its proposition in things? It is imperative to agree that all these absolutes of logic are valid for the mind and only for the mind. We say the mind, not the soul, because the soul does not experience logical necessities except when it handles ideas, and ideas are only our representations of a reality that contains more than our ideas ever suspect.

Today we find ourselves at a point in which geometry, far from being what it once was, the science par excellence and certainty itself, is nothing more than a convention, fruitful when applied to the reality that responds to proportion, but useless when applied, for example, to the will or to aesthetic feelings that have nothing to do with it.

The aesthetic schema is not a closed system like the logical schema for the simple reason that it gives an account, not of a simple object that any geometry discloses more or less, but of a changing reality of the spirit, richer than objective reality. This development has been called free and disinterested; this is an error, because it too has its law. To find it we go to the system of specific thought which we call the aesthetic *a priori*, which here, for the first time that I know of, is studied in isolation and is established.

The subject is almost absolute in the zone of rationality, but this is a very reduced zone of the world; because of this, reality surpasses the pictures of the Rationalist. Thus the true philosopher had better work with the aesthetic *a priori* approach, as does the poet. Its certainties are imprecise but, even so, stronger than the obvious certainty of logic, richer and not as limited, not enclosed in the conventional profile. The aesthetician achieves certainties that are defined only in terms of feeling. Our aesthetic *a priori* approach cannot contain all of reality, and if it attempts to, it is annulled, since with it we capture or consummate a miraculous moment of spiritual substance but not all the spirit.

When thinking of something beautiful I tend to introduce into it some of the melodic-rhythmic relations which give pleasure to my spiritual reality. Inevitably, then, I convert the object to the plastic if it pertains to its material, to the value of poetry if it pertains to its significance. The intellectualists see the spiritual in the logical opera-

tion; we situate it in the rhythmic-aesthetic operation, the poetic operation that disposes and arranges the object according to the loving
dynamism of the soul. It is reached through the systems of melody,
rhythm, harmony, and counterpoint, the true aesthetic *a priori* principles of the mind. These *a priori* principles have, over the precision of
logic, the advantage that the aesthetic precisions situate or locate objects
in a whole in which they are transcended, without deforming or abstracting them. . . .

The end sought by the artist—which is not to reduce reality to concepts—leads us to a full consummation. Thus the aesthetic *a priori*
cannot be a closed system, like that of dialectics, nor only unlimited
experience, like empiricism. The aesthetic consists of an orientation of
movement toward the divine state in which the Absolute is realized.

Translated by Carmen and John H. Haddox

Bibliography

All source materials, whether primary or secondary, are here grouped in a single alphabetical listing.

Ahumada, Herminio, Jr. *José Vasconcelos. Una vida que iguala con la acción el pensamiento.* México: Ediciones Botas, 1937.

Alessio Robles, Vito. *Mis andanzas con nuestro Ulises.* México: Ediciones Botas, 1938.

Bar-Lewaw, Itzhak. *Introducción crítico-biográphica a José Vasconcelos.* Madrid: Ediciones Latinoamericanas, 1965.

Basave Fernández del Valle, Agustín. "El destino de José Vasconcelos," *Revista Mexicana de Filosofía,* II, 3 (1959), 27–31.

———. *La filosofía de José Vasconcelos. El hombre y su sistema.* Madrid: Ediciones Cultura Hispánica, 1958.

Brenner, Anita. "A Critic's View," *Atlantic Monthly,* Vol. 213, No. 3 (March, 1964), 131.

Brightman, Edgar S. "Don José Vasconcelos," *Philosophy and Phenomenological Research,* 7 (1947), 433–460.

———. *Person and Reality: An Introduction to Metaphysics.* New York: Ronald Press, 1958.

Caso, Antonio, *et al. Conferencias del Ateneo de la Juventud.* México: Imprenta Lacaud, 1910.

Castro Leal, Antonio. *Páginas escogidas de José Vasconcelos.* México: Ediciones Botas, 1940.

Caturla, Brú, Victoria de. *¿Cuáles son los grandes temas de la filosofía latinoamericana?* México: Editorial Novaro, 1959.

Cocteau, Jean and Jacques Maritain. *Art and Faith.* Translated by John Coleman. New York: Philosophical Library, 1948.

Crawford, William Rex. *A Century of Latin American Thought.* Cambridge, Massachusetts: Harvard University Press, 1944.

Diego Pérez, Ismael. "Vasconcelos, o el pensamiento iberoamericano," *Revista Mexicana de Filosofía*, II, 3 (1959), 47–61.

Dulles, John W. F. *Yesterday in Mexico: A Chronicle of the Revolution*. Austin: University of Texas Press, 1961.

Fernández MacGregor, Genaro. *Carátulas*. México: Ediciones Botas, 1935.

————. *Vasconcelos*. México: Ediciones de la Secretaria de Educación Pública, 1942.

Flower, Edith. "The Mexican Revolt against Positivism," *Journal of the History of Ideas*, X (January, 1949), 115–129.

Fuller, B. A. G. *A History of Philosophy* (3rd ed.) New York: Holt, Rinehart and Winston, 1955.

Gamio, Manuel and José Vasconcelos. *Aspects of Mexican Civilization*. Chicago: University of Chicago Press, 1926.

Gaos, José. *Pensamiento de lengua española*. México: Editorial Stylo, 1945.

Guy, Alain. "José Vasconcelos et Bergson," *Revista Mexicana de Filosofía*, II, 3 (1959), 63–70.

Haddox, John Herbert. "The Aesthetic Philosophy of José Vasconcelos," *International Philosophical Quarterly*, IV, 2 (May, 1964), 283–296.

————. "José Vasconcelos: Mexican Philosopher," *The Personalist*, 43 (1962), 453–465.

Jolivet, Regis. *Man and Metaphysics*. New York: Hawthorn Books, 1951.

Kerr, Walter. *The Decline of Pleasure*. New York: Simon and Schuster, 1962.

Langer, Susanne. *Problems of Art*. New York: Charles Scribner's Sons, 1957.

Larroyo, Francisco. *La filosofía americana*. México: Universidad Nacional Autónoma de México, 1958.

Lynch, William. *Christ and Apollo*. New York: Sheed and Ward, 1960.

Magdaleno, Mauricio. *Las palabras perdidas*. México: Fondo de Cultura Económica, 1956.

Marcel, Gabriel. *Creative Fidelity*. Translated by Robert Rosthal. New York: Farrar, Straus, 1964.

Maritain, Jacques and Jean Cocteau. *Art and Faith.* Translated by John Coleman. New York: Philosophical Library, 1948.

Martínez, José Luis. "La obra literaria de José Vasconcelos," *Filosofía y Letras,* XIII, 26 (April–June, 1947), 227–239.

Maslow, Abraham. *Toward a Psychology of Being.* Princeton, New Jersey: Van Nostrand Company, 1962.

Merton, Thomas. *No Man Is an Island.* New York: Harcourt Brace, 1955.

Nicotra di Leopoldo, G. T. "José Vasconcelos: el hombre y el filósofo," *Todo,* No. 1398 (July 23, 1964), 28–29.

Nieva, Rodolfo. "Vasconcelos 'Hispanista,'" *El Universal,* November 29, 1962.

Paz, Octavio. *The Labyrinth of Solitude.* Translated by Lysander Kemp. New York: Grove Press, Inc., 1961.

Ramos, Samuel. *Historia de la filosofía en México.* México: Imprenta Universitaria, 1943.

Robles, Oswaldo. "José Vasconcelos," *Revista Mexicana de Filosofía,* II, 3 (1959), 9–17.

———. "José Vasconcelos, el filósofo de la emoción creadora," *Filosofía y Letras,* XIII, 26 (April–June, 1947), 211–225.

Romanell, Patrick. "Bergson in Mexico: A Tribute to José Vasconcelos," *Philosophy and Phenomenological Research,* XXI, 4 (June, 1961), 501–513.

———. *Making of the Mexican Mind.* Lincoln, Nebraska: University of Nebraska Press, 1952.

———. *El neo-naturalismo norteamericano.* México: Universidad Nacional Autónoma de México, 1956.

Ruiz, Ramón E. *Mexico, the Challenge of Poverty and Illiteracy.* San Marino, California: The Huntington Library, 1963.

Sánchez Reulet, Aníbal, ed. *Contemporary Latin-American Philosophy.* Albuquerque: The University of New Mexico Press, 1954.

Sánchez Villaseñor, José. "'El Pitágoras' y los orígenes del pensamiento estético vasconceliana," *Revista Mexicana de Filosofía,* II, 3 (1959), 19–25.

———. *El sistema filosófico de Vasconcelos.* México: Editorial Polis, 1939.

Santayana, George. *The Realm of Matter.* New York: Charles Scribner's Sons, 1930.

———. *Three Philosophical Poets.* Cambridge, Massachusetts: Harvard University Press, 1927.

Sewell, Edith. *The Human Metaphor.* Notre Dame, Indiana: University of Notre Dame Press, 1963.

Teilhard de Chardin, Pierre. *The Future of Man.* Translated by Norman Denny. New York: Harper and Row, 1964.

———. *The Phenomenon of Man.* Translated by Bernard Wall. New York: Harper and Brothers, 1959.

Unamuno, Miguel de. *Del sentimiento,* in *Obras completas,* IV. Madrid: A. Aguando, 1951.

———. *¿Qué es la verdad?* in *Obras completas,* III. Madrid: A. Aguando, 1951.

———. *Verdad y vida,* in *Obras completas,* III. Madrid: A. Aguando, 1951.

———. *Vida de Don Quixote y Sáncho,* in *Obras completas,* IV. Madrid: A. Aguando, 1951.

Vann, Gerald, O. P. *The Water and the Fire.* New York: Sheed and Ward, 1954.

Vasconcelos, José. *Bolivarismo y Monroísmo.* Santiago de Chile: Ediciones Ercilla, 1935.

———. *Breve historia de México.* México: Ediciones Botas, 1936.

———. *La cultura en Hispanoamérica.* La Plata, Argentina: Universidad Nacional, 1934.

———. *El desastre.* México: Ediciones Botas, 1938.

———. *Discursos 1920–1950.* México: Ediciones Botas, 1950.

———. *En el ocaso de mi vida.* México: Editorial Populibros, 1957.

———. *Estética.* México: Ediciones Botas, 1935; 3rd ed., 1945.

———. *Estudios indostánicos.* Madrid: Editorial Saturnino Calleja, 1920.

———. "Etapa de armonía," *Logos,* I, 3 (September, 1951), 20–24.

———. *Ética.* Madrid: M. Aguilar, 1932; 2nd ed., México: Ediciones Botas, 1939.

———. "Filosofía-Estética," *Filosofía y Letras,* XIII, 26 (April–June, 1947), 197–209.

———. *La flama: los de arriba en la revolución, historia y tragedia.* México: Compañía Editorial Continental, 1959.

———. *Hernán Cortés, creador de la nacionalidad.* México: Ediciones Xóchitl, 1944.

————. *Historia del pensamiento filosófico.* México: Ediciones de la Universidad Nacional Autónoma de México, 1937.

————. "El hombre y la diversidad de la naturaleza," *Revista Mexicana de Filosofía,* I, 2 (1958), 5–12.

————. *Indología.* Barcelona: Agencia Mundial de Librería, 1927.

————. *Lógica orgánica.* México: El Colegio Nacional, 1945.

————. *Manual de filosofía.* México: Ediciones Botas, 1940.

————. *A Mexican Ulysses.* Translated by William Rex Crawford. Bloomington: Indiana University Press, 1963.

————. *Monismo estético.* México: Editorial Cultura, 1918.

————. "Nacionalismo y universalismo filosóficos," *La Antorcha,* I, 8 (November, 1931), 18–27.

————. *Obras completas.* 4 vols. México: Libreros Mexicanos Unidos, Vol. I, 1957; Vol. II, 1958; Vol. III, 1959; Vol. IV, 1961.

————.*Pitágoras, una teoría del ritmo.* La Habana: Cuba Contemporánea, 1916.

————. *El proconsulado.* México: Ediciones Botas, 1939.

————. *¿Qué es el comunismo?* México: Ediciones Botas, 1936.

————. *¿Qué es la revolución?* México: Ediciones Botas, 1937.

————. *La raza cósmica.* Barcelona: Agencia Mundial de Librería, 1925.

————. *El realismo científico.* México: Filosofía y Letras, 1943.

————. *La revulsión de la energía.* México: Editorial Cultura, 1924.

————. *De Robinsón a Odiseo.* Madrid: M. Aguilar, 1935.

————. *Simón Bolívar.* México: Ediciones Botas, 1940.

————. "La tarea del pensamiento," *La Antorcha,* I, 10–11 (January–February, 1932), 21–24.

————. *Temas contemporáneos.* México: Editorial Novaro, 1956.

————. *Todología.* México: Ediciones Botas, 1952.

————. *La tormenta.* México: Ediciones Botas, 1936.

————. *Tratado de metafísica.* México: Editorial México Joven, 1929.

————. *Ulises criollo.* México: Ediciones Botas, 1936.

Vasconcelos, José and Manuel Gamio. *Aspects of Mexican Civilization.* Chicago: University of Chicago Press, 1926.

Villegas, Abelardo. "La filosofía de José Vasconcelos," *Revista Mexicana de Filosofía,* II, 3 (1959), 33–45.

————. *La filosofía de lo Mexicano.* México: Fondo de Cultura Económica, 1960.

Washington Vita, Luis. "José Vasconcelos (1882–1959)," *Revista Mexicana de Filosofía,* II, 3 (1959), 71–75.

Index